PLAYING CAR
AND FORTU___ ___

THE MAGI METHOD

BY

J. G. MAGI

LEGAL NOTICE

CONTENTS

3

The Box Spread

CHAPTER 1

THE MAGI METHOD

The Magi Method is an original system of fortune telling with ordinary playing cards initially developed for my personal use after practicing and becoming proficient at many systems of fortune telling which utilize mundane objects such as cards, coins, eggs, stones or tea leaves.

Fortune telling is the act of divination which employs the use of any mundane tool to obtain divine wisdom. Cartomancy is divination specifically employing the use of cards. Divination is any systematic method employed to ascertain divine guidance on a specific issue of interest or situation.

Ordinary playing cards paint an accurate picture of our world on many levels.

4 SEASONS - 4 CARD SUITS
52 WEEKS IN A YEAR - 52 CARDS IN A DECK
(2 JOKERS ADDED)
13 LUNAR CYCLES A YEAR - 13 CARDS IN EACH SUIT

The act of fortune telling with playing cards reflects very much the energy of the world we live in and also reflects a holistic, feminine, earth orientation as do all psychic and prophetic activities. This feminine orientation is balanced by the very analytical, focused, masculine energies present in the individual cards. Read accurately, playing cards represent a perfect balance of masculine and feminine energies in concert with the earth and the entire universe around us.

Most or even all modern forms of fortune telling with cards may find their roots in the use of ordinary playing cards including Tarot, Lenormand, Gypsy cards, Angel cards and countless others. Madame Lenormand who became famous for accurately foretelling the fortunes of Napoleon Bonaparte used a deck of 36 ordinary playing cards upon which she wrote various definitions, symbols and words. There is now a popular fortune telling system of 36 cards named after her.

Like the famous Madame Lenormand, we will write our meanings directly on our "practice deck" of cards to assist our learning process. We will use our unmarked "seekers deck" for our actual readings.

Fortune telling with ordinary playing cards may seem more difficult without the colorful pictures and words artistically drawn and spoon fed to the fortune teller. Instead, like a great novel, these images are limited only by your imagination. Additionally, the "practice deck" repeatedly touched and written upon by your own hand strongly carries the energy of its creator – you. You will find this to be an enormous advantage in terms of accuracy and depth of insight provided by the deck you create with your own hands over any deck created by another regardless of the skill of the artist.

Another advantage of fortune telling with ordinary playing cards over other card divination systems is that you can purchase a deck of your choosing inexpensively in any convenient store. Your unmarked seekers deck can also be used in public for fortune telling and without the obvious difference in perception of this ordinary card deck from other colorful fortune telling decks.

"FOR ENTERTAINMENT PURPOSES ONLY"

All fortune telling, psychic readings and divination services in our day are prefaced by the disclaimer that these services are "For Entertainment Purposes Only" meaning that any actions taken on the part of or interpretations made as a result of the divination are taken solely at the risk of the client.

This legal strategy to avoid liability has given fortune telling in our day the feel of a carnival side show. It conjures the image of a beggarly old gypsy woman reading cards out of the back of a horse drawn caravan wagon. She will tickle your ears with sweet lies, take your money, and be gone before sunrise. It gives the impression that fortune telling is something unsavory; that you are being tricked or robbed or lured in an elaborate con game where you are the mark.

The art and science of fortune telling through divination, on the other hand, is as old as human kind itself. Historically, divination was reserved as the secret knowledge of kings, priests and the highest governing officials. For our purposes, the words fortune telling and divination are interchangeable. If a difference may be discerned between them then fortune telling is a less formal, less ritualistic method of obtaining divine wisdom than it's twin sister divination.

The three Magi present at the birth of the savior Jesus Christ are a good example of fortune telling or divination through astrology. These men named Gaspar, Melchior and Balthazar brought gold, frankincense and myrrh to celebrate the birth of the king of kings. These men are alternatively called the three wise men and the three kings. The word "magi" forms the root of the modern words magic and magician in our day.

These three "Magi" were Astrologers, which is according to Webster: The *divination* of the influences of stars on the events and lives of persons (fortune telling). They followed a new star appearing in the sky, and additionally read and interpreted prophetic texts not included in the biblical canon and long lost to us. Attendance at that most auspicious birth besides these three Magi was limited to a few illiterate shepherds and some livestock. No priest, Levite or high priest attended the birth of the Christ.

Another historical example of the use of divination and fortune telling comes from the biblical Old Testament book of Daniel the prophet, chapter 5, verse 11: "There is a man in your kingdom having the spirit of the holy gods in him. In the time of your father he was found to have insight and intelligence and wisdom like that of the gods. King Nebuchadnezzar your father - your father the king, I say - appointed him chief of the *magicians, enchanters, astrologers and diviners*. This man Daniel…"

Of note is the fact that the words divination, magic, astrology and enchantment are all used in the same breath because they all grow from the same root.

The prophet Daniel is widely regarded by the followers of the three monotheistic religions as one of the greatest prophets of the Old Testament. He is most widely known for his loyalty and devotion to the God of the Hebrews as recounted in the famous stories of Daniel in the lions' den and Daniel in the fiery furnace. Daniel was twice sentenced to a horrible death for his unfailing devotion to the God of the Hebrews and his refusal to dishonor his faith or bend the knee to any other god.

Nebuchadnezzar in his day was the king of Babylon, perhaps the wealthiest and most powerful kingdom in the world during that age. Babylon is frequently referenced in the Bible as a representation of worldly wealth, influence and corruption. Daniel was his chief administrator and governor of this large and powerful kingdom on the earth under the powerful Babylonian king Nebuchadnezzar. Therefore, Daniel was very likely the second most powerful man on earth during his lifetime or by comparison, easily more powerful than the president of the United States of America.

Historically, kings considered themselves divine by blood line. King Nebuchadnezzar was no exception to this rule and erected a famous golden image of him self and demanded upon penalty of death to be worshiped as the only true god. Kings surrounded themselves with magi exactly equivalent to the three Magi present at the birth of the Christ. Daniel first came to be noticed by the king when he correctly interpreted the king's dream when none of the other Magi in the kingdom could do it.

Many important issues passed before the king's officials on a daily basis including building projects, food distribution, security, uprisings, and countless others. These issues were discussed and debated among the officials and the decisions were made and reported to the king for his literal *stamp* of approval. The stamp was an image worn as a ring by only the king and stamped onto each document that he approved as law. These procedures are more or less still followed to this present day.

The primary difference in decision making in our day is essentially the enforced ideological separation of church and state. During the age of the kings, each of the highest officials around the table was carefully chosen for their knowledge, wisdom and most of all spiritual gifts because the king was a god and those closest to him must demonstrate special communion with the divine. Foremost among those gifts was divination and fortune telling or ascertaining and communicating the will of the gods through mundane tools such as astrology, coins, casting of lots and later (when invented) cards. Every important decision was made with the assistance of various forms of divination or fortune telling before presentation to the king for final approval. As chief of the *diviners* and fortune tellers, Daniel's was the deciding vote on the interpretation of all divinations and fortunes cast. So, if ten important decisions passed before the king's advisers in a day, then at least forty divinations would be cast in consideration of these ten decisions. That's just one day.

Daniel, the second most powerful man on planet earth during his lifetime, rightly considered by the three great monotheistic religions to be one of the wisest and greatest prophets of all time, who lived a pure and holy life devoted to God spent his days on this earth practicing divination, fortune telling, astrology and magic.

Divination according to Webster is the art or practice that seeks to foresee or foretell future events or discover hidden knowledge usually by the interpretation of omens or by the aid of supernatural powers. Another simpler definition is that divination is the act of determining the will of God using mundane tools and symbols such as ordinary playing cards.

Another excellent example of divination or fortune telling from the Bible is King David. The man Jesus Christ is a direct blood descendant of King David. Before going into every battle, David called for the "ephod" to perform the divination and inquire of the Lord. The ephod consisted of two stones called urim and thummim which were detachable from the priest's robes and cast like lots. There are many Bible passages recounting David's extensive question and answer sessions with God using this fortune telling method now lost to us. David notably failed to use this fortune telling method only one time before going into battle. His battle hardened troops were routed and he lost some of his best and strongest men in a battle that David had considered an easy victory and not even worthy of his attention. When David went with tears before the Lord to ask why, God instructed him to never again trust only in his own strength and cunning by neglecting to perform the divination before going into battle.

Fortune telling and divination through the use of ordinary playing cards is not a trick, a silly game or a carnival side show but the secret knowledge of many of the wisest and most influential persons ever to walk on planet earth.

A PICTURE OF THE WORLD

Every fortune telling method is a representative picture of the universe and man's journey as a physical person, spirit and eternal soul traveling through it. Utilizing a mere 54 cards (52 cards plus one red and one blue joker) we must accurately represent every shade of human experience and thinking. This is quite a challenge and often fortune telling systems fall short; some methods error on the side of being too positive and some methods error on the side of being too negative.

In the original playing card fortune telling system presented in this book I have intentionally designed a balanced approach that equally represents positive and negative as well as masculine and feminine energies.

An ordinary deck of playing cards obtained from any local convenience or corner store naturally represents the range of polarities represented by the human experience in the four traditional playing card suits. Hearts represent very pure energy. They symbolize love, kindness, emotions and spirit. But this energy is very watery and changeable and lacks the solidity and physicality to endure on its own. As we progress through the suits to diamonds and clubs, we find this solidity. We find these emotions and impulses worked out in the physical plane of existence until we reach the spades. Spades represent the polar opposite energy of the hearts suit. If the energy of the hearts suit is very pure and loving and spiritual, then the energy of the spades suit is equally impure, hateful and even destructive. An example of this is the jack of hearts (Jh). The symbol of the Jh is the Angel; pure, loving, kind, generous, and helpful. On the opposite energetic pole is the jack of spades (Js). The symbol of the Js is the Devil; evil, deceptive, selfish, and a liar.

We may find it unpleasant, uncomfortable or even unpopular to recognize the darker energies represented in our physical and spiritual world, but more importantly, this is an accurate picture of the world in which we live and the energies present. As much as 54 cards can, represented here are the full range of energies present in our world.

Accurate fortune telling with playing cards is as simple as identifying the energies present in the 13 numbers and four suits and then reading them in combination.

PRACTICE DECK & SEEKERS DECK

This is a work book. I am going to teach you fortune telling with ordinary playing cards.

STEP 1: Buy two ordinary decks of playing cards. On one set of playing cards you will write the meanings. This will be your practice deck. The other set of playing cards you will not write upon them. This will be your seekers deck.

STEP 2: Take your new decks with you everywhere. The act of creating your practice deck by writing on it and handling it transfers your spiritual energy to it. Reading with your seekers deck energizes this deck. Your practice and seekers decks become linked to your energy and thus read specifically for you. I find it takes some time for a deck to link to me and become loyal (usually about two weeks). In the beginning, as you work through this book, I advise you to take both of your decks with you everywhere, in your purse, your backpack or your briefcase. Set them beside you while you sleep. It's very important that your decks get to know you.

STEP 3: Write the key word at the top of each card. You may choose to write more than one meaning on each card of your practice deck. However, all meanings for the cards are based on the single key word provided. No matter how many meanings are written on your practice deck, the cards will always reveal new shades of meaning and surprises as your intuition and skill develop.

STEP 4: Practice, practice, practice. The book is broken up into sections of twelve cards each. The first section is cards ace through three. The second section is cards four through six and so on until we cover all 54 cards and their meanings. At the end of each section, we will practice with the cards and meanings revealed. We will do ten card pairings and five three card spreads to work with the meanings, our memory and intuition. I also encourage you to begin asking your cards at least one question a day.

THE CARTOMANCERS CREED

"This is my practice deck. This is my seekers deck. There are many others exactly like my seekers deck especially in Las Vegas, but this one is mine.

My practice and seekers decks are my trusted friends. I must master them as they will assist me to master my own life and help others on their journey. Apart from me, my practice deck and seekers decks are nothing.

I promise to interpret my seekers deck accurately. My seekers deck knows that what matters not are how many readings I cast on the same subject but how accurate and useful is each reading. I promise not to cast readings over and over on the same subject until I receive the answer I wish to hear. I promise not to sugar coat my readings for myself or others. I promise to counsel both myself and others with compassion, love and understanding as I interpret the clear messages given by the cards.

I will keep my practice and seekers decks clear from negative spirits."

Chapter 2

THE ENERGY OF THE CARDS

THE PLAYING CARD NUMBERS
ACE - New beginning; decision
TWO - Union; partnership; division
THREE - Working together; conflict
FOUR - Foundation; death
FIVE - Change
SIX - Relationships
SEVEN -Cycle of return; spirit, burden
EIGHT - Abundance; money; health
NINE - Final actions
TEN - Completion; success; journey
(11) JACK - new situation; new person
(12) QUEEN - relationships among people; global perspective
(13) KING - getting things done; taking charge; focused energy

We will examine the energies of each number in much greater detail as we work our way through each of the 54 playing cards.

THE PLAYING CARD SUITS

HEARTS ENERGY
- Love
- Happiness
- Emotions
- Relationships
- Bonding
- Desire
- Connection
- Matters of the heart
- Honesty
- Good intentions
- Creativity
- Healing
- Blood
- Life
- Faith
- Hope
- Spirit

Hearts are represented by the element of water. They are the most flexible and changeable of the four suits. The energy they represent is very fleeting and temporary and all by themselves will not maintain their resonance through the trials of life. In other words, love not backed up by concrete actions will fade; good intentions and compassion without the follow through of putting "your money where your mouth is" will not make a material difference in the world or in another person's life. At their worst, Hearts on their own, unsupported by the more substantial energies represented in the other suits can be nothing more than wishes, good intentions or the proverbial "bleeding heart" of all talk and no action.

More positively, hearts represent the purest energy of all the suits. A marriage without love is a chore or worse. Sex without desire can become twisted into something very different than love. Hearts represent the ideals for which we strive as humans. Hearts represent prayer, angels, the Holy Spirit and the workings of God. Hearts represent bodily healing, the life sustaining blood in our veins and the literal heart that pumps blood through our body.

Hearts represent the joy of the physical life. Giving and receiving love, friends and other close relationships. Hearts represent partying the night away and drinking too much. Hearts represent the spark of creativity, inspiration and the pure spark of passion in human relationships and in any field of endeavor.

DIAMONDS ENERGY

- Money
- Investments
- Physical comforts
- Food
- Shelter
- Transportation
- Material success
- Manifestation on the material plane
- Technology
- Communication
- Contracts
- Legal judgments

Diamonds represent a combination of earth and fire energy. As the energy progresses through the suits from hearts to diamonds to clubs to spades, the energy represented by each suit slows until it reaches the spades where the energy of the spades is a road block, stagnant or even destructive. Here in the diamonds suit, the energy is still very fast but also very solid and material.

Diamonds represent money, physical goods of material value which can be as literal as diamonds and the finer things in life. A car, a job, a home, a bank account and stock investments may all be represented here. Fine dining, extravagant vacations, success and the material abundance of life are also here. Diamonds manifest the pure desires of the hearts suit into this material reality.

Diamonds also represent legal contracts such as business partnerships, marriage and all forms of financial obligations. Diamonds also symbolize electricity and all forms of communication via cell phones, email, postal mail and face to face communications.

CLUBS ENERGY
- Growth
- Hard work
- Mundane details of life
- Progress through effort
- Structure
- Nurture
- Earth
- Stable
- Grounded
  Yin

Clubs energy is very stable, rooted and foundational. Clubs energy reflects earth energy in its purest expression. This is life on the physical plane. Clubs energy is grounded and immensely practical. It gets the job done and moves forward on to the next task on the "to do" list. Clubs energy is yin energy which is very passive and unmoving. All progress that is made grows out of the solid structure and foundation of what already exists and is relatively unchanging from day to day. Clubs energy is like a farmer sowing his field with corn. He works hard to sow the seeds in the field. Then he waits. Several months later, the fields will be bursting with the corn that he worked hard to plant. If he comes every day to look, he may see no difference at all in his fields. If he is foolish enough to dig up the seeds he planted, then he will have nothing to show at harvest time. The earth turns on its own schedule. The seeds grow without any human intervention. In between the sowing and the harvest, there are endless other things he must do to maintain his farm and get ready for the reaping, storing and sale of his corn. But the farmer doesn't make the corn grow. The earth is alive and the seed is alive and all of it interacts to create on its own schedule. Mankind also is part of the ecosystem and plays his role. This is clubs energy.

SPADES ENERGY

- Conflict
- Pain
- Loss
- Illness
- Endings
- Negativity
- Destruction
- Death
- Deception
- Judgment
- Decisions
- Reasoning
- Logic
- Saturn
- Restriction
- Addiction
- Anxiety
- Confinement
- Unclean spirits

Spades are the polar opposite energetically of the hearts suit. Spades are ruled by the element air and roughly correspond to the swords in tarot. By the time the energy reaches the spades suit it has reversed its natural positive flow and works restriction, chaos, destruction and pain wherever it goes. When something ends, something new begins; when something dies, something else is born. The vacuum left by the person, thing or activity that dies is naturally filled by something different, something better, and often something stronger. We cannot have what is superior until we let go of what is inferior.

Spades clear out the dead things in our lives. They are the vultures, undertakers and reapers. Death is painful. Loss is never an enjoyable undertaking.

Spades represent the natural cycle of decay, pruning and death that is essential to the life cycle of any healthy organism, microcosm and macrocosm.

Chapter 3

BEGINNINGS, COUPLES AND GROWTH
ACE, TWO AND THREE

THE ACE. The Ace represents new beginnings. Just as the first light of the sun peeks over the horizon and a new day dawns, the ace represents the beginning of this suit energy coming to bear in the situation described by the cards. As a rule, the ace represents the energetic qualities of all of the cards bearing the same suit. The ace also represents the purest energy of the suit itself. The ace is like a seed from which the tree of the cards grows and develops.

ACE OF HEARTS
HEART

Write "Heart" at the top of the ace of hearts on your practice deck. The word "Heart" is the symbol of this card. The additional definitions below are subordinate adjectives which describe the symbol. As you practice and develop your skills and intuition as a fortune teller, you may or may not choose to write additional meanings on your practice deck at your discretion. The quickest and easiest road to fortune telling genius is to assign one primary meaning to each card and memorize it. All other listed meanings are subordinate to this one definition.

The Heart represents a positive out flowing of emotions as well as a person's emotional response to another person or circumstance depending on the surrounding cards. The Heart can represent the love between married couples, the excitement of a new relationship, the unconditional love of a parent toward a child or even the love of a master for his/her pet or even vice versa.

The ace corresponds to the number one. Hearts are very pure energy and correspond to the element of water. They represent spirit, love and emotions. They are pure but they also shift and change easily unless they land beside cards that represent more solid energies.

The Heart card in readings may also represent joy, happiness, passion, compassion, blessing, gift, charity, connection, honesty, pure intentions, unconditional love, the physical heart and physical health.

ACE OF DIAMONDS
SUN

Write this meaning at the top of the corresponding card in your practice deck.

The symbol of the ace of diamonds is the Sun. The Sun is the giver of life on planet earth. Everything prospers in the light of the sun. Whatever falls beside the Sun card is blessed.

Aces represent beginnings. This ace represents the beginning of prosperity, a new idea or good fortune. As a member of the diamond suit, this ace represents money and all the things money can buy. Therefore, the success, warmth and illumination this card brings translate directly to the material world.

The Sun card in readings may also represent clarity, insight, illumination, blessing, good fortune, no hidden agenda, sun, Son (of God), God's love, God's favor, beginning of a time of tremendous growth and success, summer and warmth.

ACE OF CLUBS
MUSTARD SEED

Write this meaning at the top of the corresponding card in your practice deck.

The symbol of the ace of clubs is the Mustard Seed. Jesus said, "If you have faith as small as a mustard seed, you can say to this mountain, 'Move from here to there' and it will move." The Mustard Seed is among the smallest of seeds but when planted grows to an enormous size. The lesson of the Mustard Seed is that things that seem very small may grow to become very big things.

All clubs energy grows out of the existing situation. The Mustard Seed is a part of the situation already and it is looking for an opportunity to grow. The Mustard Seed in a reading represents the beginning of a new situation, planting the seed, new idea, inspiration, power, creativity, spark, opportunity, potential, faith, prayer, spiritual sign or vision.

The Mustard Seed also represents messages or documentation in any form such as a letter, legal paper, will, email, text, phone call, secret, gossip around the water cooler at work, news paper or blog. However the message is conveyed, important new information is imparted to the recipient.

ACE OF SPADES
STRAIGHT RAZOR

Write this meaning at the top of the corresponding card in your practice deck.

The symbol of the ace of spades is the Straight Razor. The Straight Razor cuts away what has served its purpose and must go. The Straight Razor may describe the breakup of a relationship, the ending of a business contract, the dissolution of a marriage or a physical separation. The Straight Razor may describe a wound, injury or accident. The Straight Razor may also describe the surgeon's knife.

The Straight Razor in readings may also represent a cut, wound, injury or something emotionally painful. The action of the Straight Razor is fast and immediate.

MULTIPLE ACES APPEARING IN A READING

Fortune telling with playing cards is unique from other fortune telling card systems in that multiple cards of the same number and different suit (multiples) will commonly appear in a reading where spirit is attempting to get a message across to the seeker and the course of action is quite clear. Multiples appearing in a reading should cause the seeker to pay closer attention.

Aces are about new beginnings. Each suit represents a different area of life. Hearts represent love, emotions and spirit. Diamonds represent money and physical comforts. Clubs represent a new directions, situations and important information. Spades represent an important decision or a sudden accident.

If all four aces appear together in a reading then every area of life will be affected decisively and immediately by a new beginning or fresh start such as relocation, marriage or immigration to a new country.

If three aces appear in a reading, with the exception of the ace of spades then the reading indicates an important message has been received or will very soon be received auguring a new beginning in the areas of love and money such as an important job that will cause the seeker to relocate or a marriage engagement.

If the ace of spades and the ace of diamonds appear together in a reading, then an important decision must be made concerning money.

The multiples increase their influence on the reading as more of the same number appears in the reading.

THE TWO. The two represents partnerships and people teaming up together or breaking apart. "Two are better than one because they have a good return for their work. If one falls down, his friend can help him up." Song of Songs 4:9-10. Humans are social animals and must naturally band and work together to both survive and thrive.

TWO OF HEARTS
LOVERS

Write this meaning at the top of the corresponding card in your practice deck.

The symbol of the two of hearts is the Lovers. Two hearts beat as one. These two have an emotional bond with each other. This emotional bonding can occur between two married people, a dating couple, Lovers or even between an owner and his/her pet. In other words, the owner feels love for his pet and/or vice versa depending on the question asked. This card can also indicate the sexual act or coupling. Because this card belongs to the heart suit, the energy of this card assigns to the element of water and the emotions and feelings may change quickly.

The Lovers card in a reading may represent a sweetheart, a crush, flirting, physical attraction, dating or the 'apple of my eye'. This card can also represent any particularly loving platonic relationship between two parties. The emphasis in the Lovers card lies more heavily upon the feelings than any actions. The Lovers card indicates a particular fixation by one or both parties upon the other.

TWO OF DIAMONDS
DIAMOND RING

Write this meaning at the top of the corresponding card in your practice deck.

The symbol of the two of diamonds is the Diamond Ring. The most obvious interpretation of the Diamond Ring is the bond of marriage. The Ring is an unbroken circle and it represents a life long commitment to the other. The Ring also symbolizes any committed or contractual relationship backed up by law.

The Diamond Ring in readings may also represent partnership, contract, responsibility, an offer, connection, jewelry, small expensive items or a circle.

TWO OF CLUBS
HANDCUFFS

Write this meaning at the top of the corresponding card in your practice deck.

The symbol of the two of clubs is Handcuffs. Anyone found in Handcuffs typically is not wearing them willingly. Someone else, usually a police officer, has placed these bracelets on them by force against the will of the wearer. Someone forced to work on a team with someone they don't know, have no personal feelings for or even dislike is Handcuffs. Sitting beside a stranger on a plane; meeting someone for a blind date and feeling no connection or interest; a partnership or marriage long dead of any passion. This is the image of Handcuffs.

Handcuffs indicate a union without any emotional feelings or slightly negative feelings that are not acted upon; yoked together; feeling forced or duty bound to interact with this other party. It is important for the seeker to note that if they believe this relationship with this other party to be close, personal or loving; the appearance of this card in a reading indicates a lack of mutual feelings, a lack of caring or possibly the existence of slightly negative emotions toward the seeker. The appearance of Handcuffs also indicates a purely professional, clinical or impersonal relationship.

Handcuffs in readings may represent the number two; two eyes, two breasts, two testacies, two lungs, two hands, twins or any combination of the number two.

TWO OF SPADES
BROKEN CHALICE

Write this meaning at the top of the corresponding card in your practice deck.

The symbol of the two of spades is the Broken Chalice. A golden cup now rendered completely useless due to a giant crack down one side. The chalice once highly treasured is now useless as a container.

The Broken Chalice may appear in a reading when a married couple divorces, an unmarried couple breaks up and goes their separate ways or a former friend becomes an enemy.

The Broken Chalice in readings also represents a bad relationship, disharmony, discord, imbalance, a break up, split, opposition, separation, fighting, an enemy, misunderstanding and incompatibility.

By the time the energy reaches the spades suit the energy has stopped and reversed itself and now lies in direct opposition to the positive aspects of the card.

MULTIPLE TWOS APPEARING IN A READING

The two represents partnerships. Multiple twos appearing in a reading indicate either multiple partnerships or a single partnership affecting multiple areas of the seekers life simultaneously. Pay attention to how many red versus black twos appear. More spades and clubs may indicate a more negative or slower energy where more hearts and diamonds may indicate a faster energy with more emotional charge.

THE THREE. The three represents growth, improvement and increase, working together and activity.

THREE OF HEARTS
ROSES

Write this meaning at the top of the corresponding card in your practice deck.

The symbol of the three of hearts is Roses. Roses are an unexpected surprise. Roses symbolize love and passion. This gift is given with a pure heart.

Roses represent a gift, surprise, pregnancy, bearing the fruit of your labors, a new baby, vagina, literal flowers, an attractive female, Mary the mother of Jesus who comes preceded by the sweet scent of roses, the presence of God's angels, the Holy Spirit and the color red.

THREE OF DIAMONDS
TRINITY

Write this meaning at the top of the corresponding card in your practice deck.

The Trinity is an obvious reference to the Father, Son and Holy Ghost of Christianity. Although each is a separate and distinct personality with differing duties and individual will, they stand perfectly united in purpose. They are literally one.

The diamonds suit is an excellent expression of this energy since the diamonds are very material and energy appearing in the diamonds suit is always worked out on the physical plane.

The Trinity may appear in a reading when people are working together; when circumstances are all falling into place toward a common goal and when a group of people are united by a common interest. The Trinity emphasizes cooperation, teamwork and alliances.

The Trinity in readings may also represent a work group, a Bible study, a support group such as alcoholics anonymous, a social club, a sports team, a group of close friends, three, Father, Son and Holy Ghost, a family or more than one other supportive extended family member.

THREE OF CLUBS
THREE BLACK BIRDS

Write this meaning at the top of the corresponding card in your practice deck.

The symbol of the three of clubs is Three Black Birds. Three Black Birds always fly in a group. They are very social, they pass the news and chatter along the grape vine having all the latest gossip. Three Black Birds can represent business people, business meetings, negotiations, the frenetic activity of the business world and getting things done. These are busy people sharing and transmitting interesting information.

Three Black Birds in readings may also represent a job interview, chatting on social media, texting, tweeting, posting, phone conversations, negotiations, meeting for coffee with friends, exercise, jogging, playing sports, teams and physical activity.

THREE OF SPADES
SCOURGE

Write this meaning at the top of the corresponding card in your practice deck.

The symbol of the three of spades is the Scourge. The Scourge is an instrument of punishment, suffering and vengeance. The Scourge does not strike just one time but again and again and again. The cumulative effect of the strikes causes the pain. The Scourge is ongoing, repetitive and relentless.

The Scourge may appear in the reading as a conflict flaring up or unresolved, a heart break or someone interfering between two others. The Scourge may represent the "odd man out", three is a crowd, a love triangle, others working against you or people talking behind your back.

The Scourge may represent a disease, infestation or chronic illness. Spiritually, the Scourge may represent the activities of witchcraft, demons, curses and addictions.

The Scourge when present in a situation causes pain, interference and conflict from so many directions at once that it becomes almost the environment itself.

MULTIPLE THREES APPEARING IN A READING

Threes represent expansion, increase, working together and bearing fruit from your labors.

If all four threes appear together in a reading then there exists the burgeoning expansion of something new that has come into your life affecting every aspect of your existence. A good example, but only one of endless possibilities, is the birth of a first child. Up until this point this couple was single. They enjoyed volleyball, skiing and traveling internationally. Three of hearts or Roses indicates this wonderful gift has entered their life. Three of diamonds or Trinity indicates how everything will now work toward raising this child including the fact that mom has decided to stay at home and dad will need to be more focused at work due to the substantial loss of income and the dramatic increase in expenses (three of spades) that seem to be growing every second. Three of clubs or Three Black Birds involves tremendous activity. Perhaps the dreaded mother in law has come for a month to stay in their small apartment and she bears a striking resemblance to Hitler or at least Napoleon even down to the unattended hairs on her upper lip and tucking her hand into her shirt and leaving it there at length for no apparent reason. Every aspect of existence has changed and this is just the beginning. That is the energy of four threes in a reading.

Three threes and two threes respectively indicate change and burgeoning initiative in the areas represented by the suits appearing. Diamonds are money and communication. Spades are conflict. Clubs represent activity. Hearts represent desire. Threes are just the beginning. As a situation progresses in any area of life, the cards appearing in readings will move toward ten or completion only to begin the cycle again. The energy recycles eternally. Three indicates everything is beginning to work together and the planted seeds have begun to sprout.

TEN SAMPLE CARD PAIRINGS ACE THROUGH THREE

The first and most basic spreading technique is card pairings. The relationships between the cards are very important and cards should be read in relation to the other cards around them and in relationship to the question.

Now we will work with aces through threes in some sample card pairings to see some possible meanings that could appear in readings. There are too many possible combinations to list all possible meanings for each pair or set of cards. Furthermore, the meanings vary depending on the question asked and the other cards present. For example, sometimes the cards are very literal. I once asked if I should go with friends to a bar on St Patrick's Day. In the middle was the four of clubs or the Four Leaf Clover which typically indicates good luck. However on both sides of the four of clubs were negative cards indicating I should not go with them. In this case the four of clubs or Four Leaf Clover was literally indicating Irish or St Patrick's Day as the theme of the reading. Here are some sample card pairings to get your intuition and memory working. This is a workbook, so we will do sample card pairings and three card draws at the end of each section of cards. Please try these pairings out on your own and do some others not listed for practice and learning.

Ace of hearts and two of diamonds = Heart and Diamond Ring. A relationship or marriage founded in love; a business founded in passion.

Ace of hearts and three of clubs = Heart and Three Black Birds. Light dating or gossiping about matters of the heart.

Ace of hearts and ace of diamonds = Heart and Sun. This indicates a fortunate pairing or a love that will last.

Ace of hearts and two of spades = Heart and Broken Chalice. This pairing indicates a broken relationship; a breakup or divorce; a split between friends or family members.

Ace of spades and three of spades = Straight Razor and Scourge. Put an end to a recurring problem that will only get worse if not dealt with. Remember, threes indicate a beginning of the energy represented. Three of spades or Scourge here could be a health problem, a car problem or any kind of recurring problem.

Ace of spades and three of clubs = Straight Razor and Three Black Birds. Put an end to gossip; gossip concerning an accident or talk about surgery.

Two of spades and ace of spades = Broken Chalice and Straight Razor. One split card and one cutting card; divorce; a decisive end to a relationship.

Two of spades and ace of clubs = Broken Chalice and Mustard Seed. Divorce papers; Dear John letter; nip it in the bud; fresh start after divorce or breakup.

Three of clubs and two of hearts = Three Black Birds and Lovers. Gossip about sex; locker room talk; the physical sexual act.

Three of hearts and two of diamonds = Roses and Diamond Ring. Engagement; marriage proposal; wedding reception; a beautiful union.

HOW TO READ THE THREE CARD SPREAD

The three card spread has no formal positions and as a result is very free flowing. To cast a three card spread, simply shuffle your cards while thinking about your question and lay three cards in a line.

CARD 1/ CARD 2/ CARD 3

After establishing meanings for all of the cards, I recommend that you cast at least one three card spread a day until you gain a basic familiarity with the meanings of all of your cards and their relationships to each other. The three card spread is the quickest and easiest way to get a clear answer to a question. Always ask a clear question and write it down before shuffling and casting the cards.

CARD 1 - represents the past and events leading up to the current state of affairs.

CARD 2 – represents the present. This card usually illuminates the current situation and the heart of the matter. This card will also often illuminate the emotional state of the seeker and what they are thinking and feeling. The middle card in any reading also represents the theme of the reading.

CARD 3 – represents the future and the outcome of this situation. Card 3 also may represent the advice.

THREE CARD SPREADS USING ACE THROUGH THREE

The meanings that follow are not the only possible meanings for these card combinations. There are as many meanings as there are questions and seekers. My purpose here is to get you started on your fortune telling journey and to prime the pump of intuition so that you may as quickly as possible begin reading and interpreting your own spreads. In addition to the positions listed above, it's important to read the cards in combination as pairs or triplets which represent the superior, more intuitive method of reading.

I recommend beginners to fortune telling with cards begin their journey reading three card spreads. Let's cast some sample three card spreads using Aces to threes. Try unpacking these three spreads on your own before reading the answers below.

1. A woman asks, "How will my job interview go?" She casts ace of diamonds, three of clubs and two of diamonds= Sun, Three Black Birds and Diamond Ring.

2. A fifteen year old boy asks, "What will happen if I ask Jenny to the dance? He casts ace of hearts, ace of clubs and three of spades = Heart, Mustard Seed and Scourge.

3. A twenty year old female asks, "What does my new man think of me?" She casts two of hearts, two of clubs and three of hearts = Lovers, Handcuffs and Roses.

SAMPLE ANSWERS

1. Well, how did her job interview go? Sun indicates it went great - very successfully! Three Black Birds as the middle card is the theme of the reading. Three Black Birds

is literally a job interview and people meeting and talking. Diamond Ring is contract. She got the job whether she's been informed of this yet or not.

2. What's going to happen if he asks Jenny to the dance? Heart indicates that he is smitten. Mustard Seed indicates the initiating action of him asking her out, the great potential indicated by this simple act and planting the seed or communicating his message to her. Scourge indicates a conflict or the presence of another person. She already has a date with another boy or perhaps another conflicting obligation.

3. What does he think of her? Handcuffs in the center are the theme. Handcuffs will indicate two persons yoked together without any feelings good or bad between. Handcuffs can indicate a very casual acquaintance or even a complete stranger. Lovers indicates love right? Well, Lovers may literally represent the act of sex itself. They had sex together. Added to Handcuffs, it means he has no feelings yet. Roses indicate a romantic gift or surprise. Roses can also represent a woman's vagina. So read as a sentence these cards say, they had a romantic sexual encounter. However, her question was how does he feel about her? Handcuffs indicate he doesn't yet have any romantic or even friendship feelings toward her. More information is likely in order. Does he have a girlfriend? There are many card spreads we can employ to find out more about the situation. We will cover more spreads as we learn the cards and also at the end of the book.

Chapter 4

FOUNDATION, CHANGE AND RELATIONSHIPS
FOUR, FIVE AND SIX

THE FOUR. A four is like a square. The four represents solidity, foundation, building blocks, four walls, a car, a bed, a coffin or a house. The number four represents the structure upon which life is built for better or worse.

FOUR OF HEARTS
HOME

Write this meaning at the top of the corresponding card in your practice deck.

The symbol of the four of hearts is the Home. Home is where the heart is and these are the individuals closest to the heart of the seeker. These are the people with whom we invest our greatest energy and time. Husbands, wives, children, pets, close friends, brothers, sisters, mothers, fathers, cousins or lovers. These are the individuals we can count on to get us through the days, weeks, years and decades of life and those whom the seeker will turn to when times get tough. We turn to them when we need advice, a shoulder to cry on, some chicken soup or a few dollars to get through the rest of the week. These individuals care deeply for us just as we care deeply for them.

Home represents an environment where we can feel safe and secure and persons who nurture and care for us.

FOUR OF DIAMONDS
CORNERSTONE

Write this meaning at the top of the corresponding card in your practice deck.

The symbol of the four of diamonds is the Cornerstone. Historically, the corner stone was the first stone set when building any brick or stone structure. After laying the cornerstone, the builders would then build around and on top of this stone so that everything following after was based on this first stone. This is likewise an important concept in the Jewish and Christian Old Testament writings. Psalm 118:22 "The stone the builders rejected has become the chief cornerstone." This passage is commonly interpreted as prophetically stating that Jesus Christ is the cornerstone and that the world has rejected his teaching as the foundation of worldly affairs. Those who follow him, however, build their lives upon the foundation he built. The four of diamonds, therefore, represents the physical things around which we build our lives in this world.

The Cornerstone in readings represents a house, a car, a job, a bank account, investments, higher education, licenses, degrees, certificates, job skills and physical items related to the number four.

Cards in the diamonds suit represent practical, tangible, solid objects and pursuits. The number four represents physical things with four walls, four wheels, solidity and stability. The diamonds suit adds the aspect of speed indicating transactions and the movement of money.

FOUR OF CLUBS
FOUR LEAF CLOVER

Write this meaning at the top of the corresponding card in your practice deck.

The symbol of the four of clubs is the Four Leaf Clover. The Four Leaf Clover is an Irish symbol of luck. This is short term luck or luck in the area questioned with the cards. Four Leaf Clover luck sprouts out of the existing circumstances spontaneously like its namesake. The Four Leaf Clover is a different kind of luck than the seven of diamonds which represents luck on a larger scale. The seven of diamonds covered in the next chapter represents the Finger of God reaching down and touching the lives of men. Four Leaf Clover luck sprouts spontaneously out of the existing circumstances whereas Finger of God luck comes down from heaven. This is earthly energy versus heavenly energy. The Four Leaf Clover represents luck that sprouts suddenly and passes quickly. It also represents a growth spurt or an opportunity.

The Four Leaf Clover in readings represents the Irish, Ireland, St. Patrick's Day, the color green, leprechauns, gambling, a lucky break, physical activity, gardening, planting, growth, getting "lucky" sexually or an opportunity to be grasped.

FOUR OF SPADES
COFFIN

Write this meaning at the top of the corresponding card in your practice deck.

The symbol of the four of spades is the Coffin. The Coffin in readings represents a major ending. This ending can be the literal death of a person close to you or the ending of a job, career, relationship or phase of your life. All endings lead after a time of grief and loss to a new beginning. Coffin is the ending.

The Coffin may also represent illness. In a reading about health, the Coffin card may warn of coming illness usually accompanied by the eight of spades or Scapegoat, the four of clubs or Four Leaf Clover, the ace of clubs or Mustard Seed or other health related cards. If Coffin appears with the ace of spades or Straight Razor in a health reading, this could indicate a surgery. In a relationship spread the Coffin indicates the end of the relationship. In a career spread the Coffin speaks of the job ending.

The Coffin in readings usually represents a major ending, taking a time out, illness, recuperating from an illness, exhaustion, break down or even death. The Coffin also represents all who have passed over or the dead, medium ship, the dark side of the spiritual realm or demons, a grave, grave yard, a funeral, stagnation, and the color black.

MULTIPLE FOURS APPEARING IN A READING

Fours are the foundation and building blocks of life. They represent family and close relationships, possessions, activity and growth and finally the end of the life cycle of growth.

If four fours appear together in a reading then the very foundations of existence will change for the seeker. Four fours is an indication of establishing an entirely new foundation. This is a different energy than the ten of spades or Earthquake which indicates the sudden destruction and annihilation of the existing foundation in a particular area of life before establishing the new foundation. Four fours may leave the previous foundation intact while establishing a completely new foundation depending on the other cards.

Three fours and two fours indicate either the solidity and stability of the existing foundation in those areas represented or establishing a new foundation in the suit areas represented. If multiple fours appear in a reading indicating a new foundation in some areas but the four of spades or Coffin also appears, then this indicates an ending in a particular ending and a concurrent beginning in the other areas.

THE FIVE. Five represents the principle of change. "The only constant in life is change," Heraclitus. Five represents a change of heart, a change of direction, a change for better or worse and the hands and feet that enact the change.

FIVE OF HEARTS
FENCE SITTER

Write this meaning at the top of the corresponding card in your practice deck.

The symbol of the five of hearts is the Fence Sitter. The Fence Sitter could go any way the wind blows and will move in whichever direction the cards before and beside indicate. The five represents change. Hearts belong to the element water. The five is also known as the hands and feet that enact change. Due to the strong water element represented in the five of hearts most of the activity takes place unseen beneath the surface. The Fence Sitter leaves all of the options open and waits for others to decide before deciding anything. If they change their minds, the Fence Sitter will change and flip positions quicker than a flash. The Fence Sitter may also change his/her mind so many times and so quickly that it makes others heads spin. The Fence Sitter does not act upon a situation but rather re-acts to the people and events acting upon that situation. The change can be positive or negative or just plain confusing. At the appearance of the Fence Sitter, the change may not yet have manifested in the physical realm. This card in some systems is called the "Fickle Woman" due to the hearts suit which is very watery and emotional.

The Fence Sitter is flexible, changeable, uncommitted, fickle, and moody. These changes can manifest positively or negatively or both simultaneously.

As a heart suit, the five of hearts also represents changes occurring in the spirit world not yet manifested on this earthly plane as in the Lord's Prayer that states "Thy will be done on the earth as it is in heaven." The Fence Sitter may represent a change that has already taken place in the heavenly realms but as yet un-manifested here on the earth.

FIVE OF DIAMONDS
JACOB'S LADDER

Write this meaning at the top of the corresponding card in your practice deck.

The symbol of the five of diamonds is Jacob 's Ladder. Jacob's Ladder refers to Genesis chapter twenty eight where the future patriarch Jacob is fleeing his father Isaac's house after stealing his brother Esau's blessing. Jacob is terrified that Esau will pursue him and kill him before he can arrive safely at his Uncle Laban's household several days journey away. During the night Jacob has a dream in which he saw a ladder resting on the earth, with its top reaching to heaven, and the angels of God were ascending and descending on it.

Jacob's Ladder in readings generally represents an improvement in an existing situation. It's worth noting that the patriarch Jacob had this dream during the lowest point of his life at the time. After waking, Jacob still faces several more days of dangerous, lonely travel through the wilderness to reach his Uncle's house. Jacob's Ladder is about a bad situation improving or knowing that God is in control and even though the situation may seem really desperate, God's angels are watching over the person and the situation and they are descending to provide help and ascending the ladder to report back to heaven the situation in real time.

Jacob's Ladder may represent prayer, guardian angels, light at the end of the tunnel, climbing back from rock bottom, steps to be completed or a plan of action. Jacob's Ladder can represent the movement of a stock up or down, birth, a literal tunnel such as a subway system or a literal ladder.

The five represents change. Diamonds impact physical, day to day mundane things like money, food, shelter, physical health, comfort and communication.

FIVE OF CLUBS
CROSSROADS

Write this meaning at the top of the corresponding card in your practice deck.

The symbol of the five of clubs is the Crossroads. The seeker is faced with a decision. Clubs represent the earth elements and foundations of our lives. This decision can relate to work, home, money, childcare or any aspect of seeker's life. We make thousands of decisions each day and the accumulated impact of these decisions determine our destiny.

Crossroads may also represent a fork in the road, a new direction, options, alternatives, multiples, a decision, a choice, an actual road or street.

FIVE OF SPADES
ROAD BLOCK

Write this meaning at the top of the corresponding card in your practice deck.

The symbol of the five of spades is the Road Block. The road forward is completely blocked and there can be no further forward movement in this direction. The seeker can wait for the road to re-open, but there's no telling how long that will be. The seeker can go back and retrace their steps, effectively abandoning the journey or the more determined seeker can attempt to reach their goal via another route by taking a detour around the Road Block. Going around the Road Block will take longer; will require more effort and resources; and may be less likely to succeed.

Road Block in a reading represents obstacles, challenges, delays, detours, feeling stuck, at an impasse, blocked, opposed, unforeseen difficulties, trouble and postponement. The Road Block may represent a person who is stubborn, big and strong, powerful, working against the seeker, or a gate keeper.

MULTIPLE FIVES APPEARING IN A READING

The five falls smack dab in the middle between one and ten and therefore represents the change point and crossroads of the energies of numbers one through four as they mature toward completion of their life cycle before recycling and beginning again.

If four fives appear together in a reading then every aspect of the seekers life is undergoing change simultaneously. Four fives does not indicate that these changes are already complete, but rather that the tipping point has been reached.

Three fives and two fives indicate reaching turning points in those areas of life and endeavor.

THE SIX. Six represents relationships. As humans living in this world, we exist in relation to other people; a spouse, children, family, friends, work associates and countless other acquaintances and strangers both seen and unseen weave the interconnected web of our daily existence. The number six represents these connections.

The purest expression of the number six is the Garden of Eden. The Garden is lush, beautiful and fruitful. It is the perfect place for humankind, animals, insects and all of God's creation to thrive. However, there is a snake in the Garden and both humankind and the Garden fell from the perfection of God's grace. In numerology, the number of the beast in the Garden and his relationship to the earth and humankind is described by the infamous number "666." How are we to understand this paradox of God's perfect Garden of interconnected relationships and the depravity of the destroyer represented simultaneously in the energy of the six?

This complex interconnected web of relationship describes the essence and meaning of human existence. No man is an island and evil does not exist within the void. Both humankind's highest good and darkest evil are represented in the number six.

SIX OF HEARTS
KARMIC RELATIONSHIP

Write this meaning at the top of the corresponding card in your practice deck.

The symbol of the six of hearts is the Karmic Relationship. Karmic Relationships are the ones that reshape us to become our higher self. Often, this process is painful or unpleasant. A Karmic Relationship may last for a limited period of time and then end and restart periodically or may be a marriage or family relationship that endures consistently throughout a person's entire life span.

Karmic Relationships may include husbands, wives, children, lovers, parents, uncles, aunts, cousins, grandparents, military buddies, work associates, bosses, employees, friends, teachers, life, close connections and pets.

The Karmic Relationship in a reading may represent a soul mate, twin flame, lover, spouse or someone returning from the past after a long absence (blast from the past). The Karmic Relationship card represents memories, nostalgia, the good old days, childhood, schmaltz, old friends, passed friends, coming to terms with the past, acceptance and forgiveness.

SIX OF DIAMONDS
HAND IN HAND

Write this meaning at the top of the corresponding card in your practice deck.

The symbol of the six of diamonds is Hand in Hand. People join hands to work together in unity without fighting or bickering. The six of diamonds represents harmony, goodwill and unity in relationship.

Hand in Hand in a reading may represent agreement, contract, rapport, compatibility, cooperation, friendship, fellowship, support, mutual goals, and peace. Hand in Hand may represent two persons, thirty persons or any number of persons acting in harmony with each other upon a situation.

SIX OF CLUBS
OLIVE TREE

Write this meaning at the top of the corresponding card in your practice deck.

The symbol of the six of clubs is the Olive Tree. An olive tree may live a very long time, is exceptionally hardy, can grow in almost any soil, grows very slowly and develops a deep root system. After the last supper, Jesus led his disciples upon the Mount of Olives where he spent time praying in an olive grove immediately before his arrest and crucifixion. The Olive Tree in the Bible represents Israel, God's chosen, the elect and His people. Tremendous pressure is applied to the olives to obtain the precious oil. Pure olive oil is used for spiritual anointing similar to the use of blessed holy water.

The Olive Tree in a reading may represent a person's roots, background, family, history, ancestors, family tree, country of origin, race, creed, clan, resume, work history, career path, criminal history, credit history, associations and awards. In health readings, the Olive Tree may represent a person's physical, spiritual or mental health, healing, blood vessels, the circulatory system, intestines, medicinal treatment, brain, advanced age or any health issue. In spiritual readings, the Olive Tree may represent the church, a church denomination, Israel, Kabala, the tree of life as well as anything long lasting, nearly impossible to eradicate and having deep roots.

SIX OF SPADES
INCUBUS-SUCCUBUS

Write this meaning at the top of the corresponding card in your practice deck.

An Incubus is a demon who comes appearing in an attractive male form to a woman while sleeping. The demon will lie upon her in the bed and will seduce her either willingly or unwillingly to have sex with him. A Succubus is a demon who comes appearing in an attractive female form to a male while sleeping. The demon will likewise seduce or rape the male for the purpose of sex. After lying sexually with the victim several times for the purpose of collecting the precious seminal fluids, the demon will spiritually attach itself very strongly to the human victim and proceed to literally suck the life out of the victim. Victims of Incubi and Succubae usually feel great exhaustion, become very ill and sometimes die from the attacks.

The Six represents relationships. Satan often comes appearing as an angel of light. There are times when someone or something entering your world may seem very attractive and enticing at first, but just behind the smile and sweetness lies something very toxic, evil and destructive. This is the energy of the Incubus-Succubus.

The Incubus-Succubus in a reading usually represents a negative, jealous, toxic, abusive, controlling, violent or destructive relationship with another person. However, Incubus-Succubus in a reading may also represent other negative relationship patterns such as alcoholism, drug addiction, anorexia, bulimia, criminal or gang associations, an abusive relationship, a negative pattern of behavior, a false friend, a narcissist, someone using you solely for their own gain, a selfish person, eroticism, sadism, masochism, a sexually transmitted disease, siren, Lilith, dark magic, spell casting, demon in disguise, spirit possession, collecting of seminal fluid, someone using you to get pregnant, or an apparent friend who is an emotional or financial black hole.

The Incubus-Succubus is a parasite feeding off the energy of the host. The solution when the six of spades appears in a reading is always to remove the Incubus-Succubus energy from the food source so that it may weaken and fall off.

MULTIPLE SIXES APPEARING IN A READING

Sixes represent important relationships that may last a lifetime; the complex interconnected web of human relational existence; the body and our family tree and also dead weight and toxic relationships.

Four sixes appearing together in a reading indicates that this is a transformational time for relationships in the life of the seeker. Perhaps they are marrying, divorcing, losing an important member of the family or moving away from home.

Three sixes or "666" appearing in a reading particularly in combination with the six of spades represents the number of the beast and can indicate that all is not what it seems and the seeker should look more carefully at the situation for indications of possible deception. A dangerous time in relationship may be indicated.

Two sixes indicate an emphasis on relationships in the card suits revealed.

TEN SAMPLE CARD PAIRINGS ACE THROUGH SIX

We now have three more cards with which to work. Let's do ten sample card pairings using all six cards now available to us.

Four of clubs and ace of diamonds = Four Leaf Clover and Sun. Luck at gambling; a very lucky day; expect good fortune today; luck that endures if the seeker takes advantage.

Four of spades and six of clubs = Coffin and Oak Tree. Poor health; illness; a death in the family.

Four of hearts and three of spades = Home and Scourge. Strife at home; a simmering conflict; family feud; family members ganging up on each other.

Five of hearts and two of hearts = Fence Sitter and Lovers. A fickle lover; a crush; a passing fancy; playing games with the seekers heart.

Ace of spades and five of clubs = Straight Razor and Crossroads. A snap decision; decisive action; a decision to move forward.

Five of spades and three of spades = Road Block and Scourge. A stubborn person who thrives on conflict; a difficult problem that requires constant attention.

Six of hearts and three of hearts = Karmic Relationship and Roses. A surprise visit from an old friend or loved one; visiting dad or mom; seeing an old lover; bumping into an old flame.

Three of hearts and six of spades = Roses and Incubus/Succubus. A one night stand; a venereal disease; the gift that keeps on giving; the "bad boy" or girl who will prove to be your undoing; a Trojan horse.

Six of clubs and two of diamonds = Olive Tree and Diamond Ring. A strong and long lasting marriage; together forever; anniversary; deep rooted bond; established business relationship.

Four of clubs and two of hearts = Four Leaf Clover and Lovers. Lucky at love; getting lucky.

THREE CARD SPREADS USING ACE THROUGH SIX

Here are some sample three card spreads using the cards ace to six. Try unpacking these three spreads on your own before reading the answers below.

1. A man asks, "Planning a trip to Las Vegas. What can I expect?" He casts five of clubs, ace of diamonds and four of clubs = Crossroads, Sun and Four Leaf Clover.

2. A man asks, "I met this girl at a bar the other night. Instant connection, Wow! We're going out again tonight. What do I need to know?" He casts two of hearts, three of spades and three of hearts = Lovers, Scourge and Roses.

3. A woman asks, "I applied for a better position at work. Will I get it?" She casts five of diamonds, three of clubs and four of spades = Jacob's Ladder, Three Black Birds and Coffin.

ANSWERS

1. What can he expect? Sun in middle as theme indicates it will be very fortunate and also very sunny weather in the desert. Crossroads is his decision whether or not to go and represents the actual traveling out on the road. Four Leaf Clover is a gambling card due to the luck of the Irish. He can expect to have a great time (Sun) and win at least a little money and perhaps more than a little with Sun present (Four Leaf Clover).

2. What does he need to know? Scourge in the center indicates she has a conflict and three of spades usually indicates the presence of a third person. In this small spread there are two 3's present. She's dating someone else or is even married. This is probably going nowhere for

him. Worst case, she may actually be using him to make her other man jealous. Watch out.

3. Will she get the job? Three Black Birds in the center indicates she will be interviewed for the position and they will discuss her qualifications for the position. Jacob's Ladder is an incremental improvement and represents her application for the better position. However, Jacob's Ladder can go up or down. Coffin at the end is the deciding card and in the outcome position. It appears that no, she will not get this position and this door will close.

Chapter 5

RETURNS, ABUNDANCE AND FINAL ACTIONS
SEVEN, EIGHT AND NINE

THE SEVEN. The seven represents return, renewal, second chances and new life. The purest expression of the number seven is the unseen spiritual world. Just as the earth is a perfectly contained biosphere where not a single drop of water or any physical matter is ever lost but all things are born, thrive, die and are recycled into new life and born again, this is the energy of the seven but carried out on a much larger scale. Seven represents the eternal recycling of energy in our universe.

If "666" represents the number of the beast, then "777" is the number of heaven or "renewal, renewal, renewal." Seven represents the spirit world, angels, God, fortune and the return of love.

SEVEN OF HEARTS
STAR OF BETHLEHEM

Write this meaning at the top of the corresponding card in your practice deck.

The symbol of the seven of hearts is the Star of Bethlehem. When the chips are down and all hope seems lost, the Star of Bethlehem appears as a beacon in the night sky for those who will follow it out of the valley of darkness. The Star of Bethlehem is the new star appearing in the sky that the three Magi followed on a long and dangerous journey to the birthplace of Jesus who was swaddled and placed in a feeding trough or manger. The Star of Bethlehem heralded the coming of God's healing in the person of Jesus who brought both literal healing and a message of reconciliation everywhere he went.

The Star of Bethlehem represents healing, wholeness, restoration, second chances and love returning. The Star of Bethlehem brings hope, recovery, peace, forgiveness, reconciliation, romance, plans, planning, the soul, the Holy Spirit, angels, fame, recognition, a new chapter, dreams, dreaming and the night sky.

SEVEN OF DIAMONDS
FINGER OF GOD

Write this meaning at the top of the corresponding card in your practice deck.

The symbol of the seven of diamonds is the Finger of God. The Finger of God refers to the painting by Michelangelo in the Sistine Chapel in Rome called the "Creation of Adam" where God breathes life into Adam the first man. The Finger of God indicates a pivotal moment where God intervenes in the affairs of men. This card is named the Finger of God and not the hand of God because the intervention of the divine may at first appear quite subtle. If the seeker does not add effort and align him or herself in agreement with the will of the divine, then the positive momentum created by the Finger of God may be lost or counter balanced by human effort.

In dice games rolling a seven is a winning combination and considered very lucky. Seven is also considered God's number. In the same way that "666" is the number of the Anti-Christ, "777" is commonly regarded as the number of the Christ. Six deals with the finite things of the earth. Seven deals with the eternal things of the spirit. Seven is incidentally the most frequent possible combination with two six sided dice and can be rolled as 1+6, 2+5, 3+4, 4+3, 5+2 and 6+1. Spiritually speaking, we can understand that the Finger of God touching our lives is not unusual but happens regularly and frequently.

The "Our Father who art in heaven" prayer is the most common Christian prayer. It states, "thy will be done on earth as it is in heaven." "As above so below" mirrors this concept. When the seven of diamonds or Finger of God appears in a reading this alerts the seeker that greater fortune smiles on them if they choose to align their will in the area indicated in the cards falling beside the Finger of God in the reading.

The seven represents return and the well that never runs dry. The diamonds suit represents money, material things and communication.

The Finger of God in a reading represents an opportunity to align the seekers will with God's plan, greater fortune, lucky 7, a lucky break, windfall, profit, miracle, manifestation of a desire, destiny, change for the better, light on the path, manna from heaven and the return of the savior.

SEVEN OF CLUBS
CROSS

Write this meaning at the top of the corresponding card in your practice deck.

The symbol of the seven of clubs is the Cross. The Cross is the ultimate symbol of pain and suffering. It is written, "Cursed is every man who hangs on a tree."

The seven is a spiritual card representing return and therefore this is a well of suffering that never runs dry. The clubs suit is of the element earth and represents the physical and practical things of earthly life.

The Cross in a reading represents burdens, troubles, hardship, suffering, pain, sorrow, regret, remorse, responsibility, sacrifice, karma, destiny, hard work, stress, difficulty, faith, prayer, good works, religious beliefs, dogma, charity, devotion, church, shrine, convent, holy place, retreat, spiritual work, priest, nun, monk, eternity, soul, selflessness and Christianity.

SEVEN OF SPADES
VEIL

Write this meaning at the top of the corresponding card in your practice deck.

The symbol of the seven of spades is the Veil. In the Jewish temple in Jerusalem there are areas clearly delineated such as the outer court, the temple grounds, the sanctuary and finally the Most Holy Place. The Most Holy Place is separated from the sanctuary by a thick curtain or Veil. The Most Holy Place is so holy that only the high priest may enter and then only one time a year on the Day of Atonement. It is said that God himself dwells behind the Veil and that if the high priest sins during his brief foray behind the Veil to offer sacrifice, he will be struck dead on the spot. No one would be able to go in and get the priests dead body in that case since they would be struck dead as well. Therefore, the high priest enters with a rope tied around his ankle in case of this emergency so that the others may drag his lifeless body out from behind the Veil without also having to enter.

In the gospels it is recorded that at the moment that Jesus gave up his spirit on the cross at Calvary, there was a great earthquake and the Veil of the temple in Jerusalem was torn in two from top to bottom.

The Veil in a reading therefore represents the hidden things of God and the more passive, receptive and feminine aspects of God such as hidden knowledge, the occult, moon energy, psychic, spiritual gifts, healing, miracles, knowing, intuition, commanding the spirits, powers of exorcism, prophecy, dreams, dream interpretation, visions, astrology, divination, fortune telling, magic, ghosts, the spirit world, mediums, shamans, native American beliefs and practices, earth magic, the unconscious mind, things not yet revealed, creativity, inspiration and mystery.

MULTIPLE SEVENS APPEARING IN A READING

Sevens represent return, renewal, second chances, new life and the unseen spiritual world.

Four sevens appearing together in a reading indicates a spiritual rebirth or literally being born again and rising up to live a new life and with a completely fresh perspective.

Three sevens or "777" is the combination indicating the return of Jesus. God has chosen to directly intervene in the affairs of the seekers world. Miracles are indicated. Prayers will be answered.

Two sevens indicate second chances and a time of important spiritual movement in the seekers life which could manifest positively or negatively depending on the combinations presented.

THE EIGHT. Eight is the card of abundance. The eight represents a whole lot of something; a lot of people; an abundance of material things; abundant joy or everything going wrong all at once.

EIGHT OF HEARTS
WATER INTO WINE

Write this meaning at the top of the corresponding card in your practice deck.

The symbol of the eight of hearts is Water into Wine. Water into Wine refers to Jesus' first public miracle at a wedding feast in Galilee where he transformed ordinary casks of water into the finest wine. Wine is symbolic of the Holy Spirit. A virtually inexhaustible supply of wine was created – more than they would ever need for this particular wedding feast. Water into Wine is a card of super abundance and transformation.

Hearts are very fast, pure energy and eights represent abundance. Water into Wine in a reading represents transformation, health, fame, notoriety, a great reputation, abundant joy, wine, drunkenness, getting high, the blood of Christ, the sacraments, a miracle, a strong heart, pride, the wedding day, a feast, a party and a large family gathering.

EIGHT OF DIAMONDS
CORNUCOPIA

Write this meaning at the top of the corresponding card in your practice deck.

The Cornucopia is commonly depicted as a giant horn overflowing with fruits, nuts and sweet smelling flowers. The Cornucopia is always full and the bounty it produces is never exhausted. According to Greek mythology, the infant Zeus had to be hidden away from his murderous father in a cave on the island of Crete with his divine attendants including his nurse maid Amalthea, a goat, who suckled Zeus. The young Zeus, not realizing his own strength, accidentally broke off one of Amalthea's horns resulting in the Cornucopia or the "horn of plenty."

The eight in the diamonds suit represents abundance in physical and material things; communication and speed is additionally indicated.

The Cornucopia in a reading represents everything money can buy and all the material comforts of life; the physical world; money, the electronic movement of money, stock trading, business, commerce, food, groceries, from fine dining to grilling on the back yard patio, clothes, house, car, physical comforts, high and low end purchases, shopping, expenses, income, luxury, feasting, over indulgence, opulence, worldly power, and influence.

EIGHT OF CLUBS
CITY

Write this meaning at the top of the corresponding card in your practice deck.

The symbol of the eight of clubs is the City. An excellent example of the City card is New York City. New York City is a very densely packed ant hill of human activity. It's the city that never sleeps. City represents the physical world populated by people, acquaintances, friends and all seven degrees of separation. The City card may appear when you post on Facebook for the whole world to enjoy your current status and photos.

The City in a reading represents the work place, a social event, a bar, social media, a gathering, a business meeting, a park, a public place, a sporting event, the opera, a seminar, meeting with friends, the world, strangers, acquaintances, and any location where large groups of people meet and interact.

EIGHT OF SPADES
SCAPEGOAT

Write this meaning at the top of the corresponding card in your practice deck.

The Scapegoat is a concept established in the Old Testament book of Leviticus where the high priest chooses a goat by divination through the casting of lots. As part of a larger atonement process for the entire tribe, the high priest is instructed to then "lay both hands on the head of the live goat and confess over it all the wickedness and rebellion" of the tribe and place them squarely on this Scapegoat. The goat is then taken away from the tribe, outside the gates of the city and released into the desert to wander taking the failings, shortcomings and sins of the tribe with it.

A Scapegoat in our day is someone who is getting blamed by others for things they didn't do, weren't involved in or may not even have any solid knowledge concerning these matters. They were more or less chosen at random as the fall guy or gal by a group of others much guiltier than themselves.

The Scapegoat in a reading represents feeling overwhelmed – everything is coming down on the seeker all at once; surrounded by false friends and enemies; a subject of malicious gossip; surrounded by troubles; left out in the cold; always the last one to get the memo; excluded from the inner circle; outside of the circle of trust; the target of surreptitious glances and the sly winking of the eye; ganged up on; set up; patsy; fall guy; betrayed; seekers actions and reputation under fire; falsely accused;

surrounded by false witnesses; exiled; excluded; outcast; disgraced; undermined and deprived.

In a health reading the Scapegoat may represent an emotional breakdown; feeling overwhelmed, depressed, paranoid; schizophrenia; bad health; a health crisis, uncontrolled spread of a disease in the body and metastasis.

MULTIPLE EIGHTS APPEARING IN A READING

The eight represents an abundance of joy, people, material things, wealth and/or overwhelming trouble.

Four eights appearing together in a reading indicates being on top of the world and a period of unsurpassed abundance in every aspect of life. Fifteen minutes of fame may be indicated.

Three eights and two eights respectively represent a time of abundance in the areas represented by the surrounding cards. As the eight of hearts may also indicate drunkenness or excessive exuberance, caution may be indicated if other negative cards are present.

THE NINE. Nine is the card of final actions. When the nine shows in a reading, the seeker has almost reached the finish line of a life journey. The goal is so close; the seeker can smell it, taste it and almost feel the exultation in their breast as they cross that line. It all comes down to one last push, a few more steps and breaching the final obstacle to achievement. Nines represent the last efforts and the final actions taken to reach an all important goal.

NINE OF HEARTS
YES

Write this meaning at the top of the corresponding card in your practice deck.

The symbol of the nine of hearts is Yes. Yes is a card of success and achievement of the seekers hearts desire. Yes represents an open door, a wish granted and all systems go. The hearts suit is very pure, acts quickly and nine represents the final act before ten and completion. There are no further obstacles present as in "ask and it shall be given" and the wish shall be granted as soon as the seeker asks.

Yes in a reading represents a wish granted, happiness, satisfaction, emotional fulfillment, success, breakthrough, access, solution, cure, open sesame, key, transformation, release and loosing.

NINE OF DIAMONDS
MERCURY

Write this meaning at the top of the corresponding card in your practice deck.

The symbol of the nine of diamonds is Mercury. The number nine indicates final actions and the diamond's suit represents communication, business and the material world. Mercury is the winged messenger of the gods who wears magical winged shoes. He represents commerce, trade, travel, communication, eloquence, messages, quick thinking, trickery and thievery.

Mercury in a reading often indicates an important person or message arriving imminently, news, delivery, letter, movement, errands, approach, vehicle, prayer, angels, communication, media, wire transfer, business, commerce, quick thinking, eloquence, lawyer, clever and mischievous.

NINE OF CLUBS
HIGH TOWER

Write this meaning at the top of the corresponding card in your practice deck.

The symbol of the nine of clubs is the High Tower. The energy of the clubs suit is very stable, slow and earthy. The clubs are in no hurry to finish and will act when they good and ready. Thus, the seeker in the High Tower retreats from the world. All the work has been done, the ducks sit lined up in nice neat rows ready for the final accounting before the energy of the tens and completion. The seeker feels exhausted and needs a respite from the world.

The High Tower may represent authority, big business, government, military, police, the justice system, university, education system, social institutions, high rise apartment, jail, quarantine and office building.

The High Tower in a reading may also represent isolation, exhaustion, spiritual retreat, contemplation, loneliness, mild depression, a period of rest, recuperation, a vacation to "get away from it all," protection, a remote location, hermit, self employed, cell tower, mountain top, upstairs, ambition, tall and the spine.

NINE OF SPADES
NO

Write this meaning at the top of the corresponding card in your practice deck.

The symbol of the nine of spades is No. The No card indicates you will not receive that for which you came. If you press forward you will get trapped in the spider's web of circumstances surrounding the object of your desire. There is also the small matter of the giant spider that spun the web you find yourself trapped within which intends to eat you. No is a stop sign. You may try again later for a better result, but at this time it's not going to work out in your favor. Attempting now brings more harm than good.

No in a reading says stop, change your mind, walk away, bad idea, getting or feeling stuck, a sticky situation, a trap, delay or spiritual binding.

MULTIPLE NINES APPEARING IN A READING

The nine represents the final actions before reaching the finish line.

Four nines appearing together in a reading indicate the finish line is in sight and a major life cycle is nearing completion as in a child leaving for university; graduation from university; joining or leaving the military; a first time mother or father.

Three nines and two nines in a reading respectively indicate approaching the finish line and wrapping up final details of a life journey indicated by the suits and the surrounding cards. The nine of spades appearing indicates that something lesser will have to be relinquished by the seeker to attain something of greater value.

TEN SAMPLE CARD PAIRINGS ACE THROUGH NINE

We now have three more cards with which to work. Let's do ten sample card pairings using all nine cards now available to us.

Seven of diamonds and four of clubs = Finger of God and Four Leaf Clover. Two luck cards representing long term luck and a short term opportunity that needs to be acted upon immediately in Four Leaf Clover. Buy a lottery ticket; take advantage of the opportunity immediately before the seeker; a short and long term shift into a better series of options.

Seven of clubs and two of diamonds = Cross and Diamond Ring. Can indicate trouble in your committed relationship or marriage; cross can indicate destiny and may indicate that seeker and their partner are destined to be together; or trouble with a business partnership.

Seven of spades and four of spades = Veil and Coffin. In a spiritual reading this combination would indicate a medium or psychic who speaks to the dead; prophesy; hidden knowledge; healing in association with the eight of hearts, ace of hearts, four of clubs or other cards.

Eight of hearts and eight of diamonds = Water into Wine and Cornucopia. The seekers 15 minutes of fame has arrived; the seeker is the toast of the town; the seeker is elected home coming queen; the seeker is admitted into Harvard; a time of overwhelming material abundance and joy is upon the seeker.

Five of diamonds and eight of diamonds = Jacob's Ladder and Cornucopia. Five of diamonds is often rock bottom or the basement landing zone after a difficult period in the seekers life. From here life is going to get much better and the seeker will enjoy a time of great abundance in multiple areas of life.

Eight of spades and four of hearts = Scapegoat and Home. The seeker loses their home; seeker is separated from those he/she loves; the seeker is disgraced in the eyes of loved ones.

Nine of hearts and three of hearts = Yes and Roses. A hoped for pregnancy; receiving exactly the gift desired; the beautiful woman says yes (Roses are feminine); a night of passion between lovers.

Nine of spades and three of diamonds = No and Trinity. Uncooperative; people not working together; others pretending to work together but passive aggressively working against the seeker or working against each other.

Nine of diamonds and five of clubs = Mercury and Crossroads. A decision is approaching very quickly and will have to be made; approaching a fork in the road; a message received providing two or more options; A road trip; someone arriving upon the situation.

Seven of spades and three of spades = Veil and Scourge. Dark magic; demonic oppression or infestation; a bad habit; unable to quit smoking; struggling with drug or alcohol addiction; a deeply rooted festering conflict.

THREE CARD SPREADS

Here are some sample three card spreads using the cards ace through nine. Try unpacking these three spreads on your own before reading the answers below.

1. A woman asks, "Will I get pregnant within the next three months?" She casts eight of hearts, three of hearts and nine of hearts = Water into Wine, Roses and Yes.

2. A man asks, "I am planning a move across the country and I am nervous to be moving away from my family. Is this a good move for me?" He casts nine of diamonds, five of clubs and eight of diamonds = Mercury, Crossroads and Cornucopia.

3. A man whose unemployment is running out asks, "When will I find another job?" He casts seven of clubs, four of diamonds and four of clubs = Cross, Cornerstone and Four Leaf Clover.

SAMPLE ANSWERS

1. Will she get pregnant within the next three months? Three of hearts or Roses in the center as theme indicates a wonderful surprise or gift and may also very literally symbolize a woman's hidden treasure. Nine of hearts = Yes; success and achievement of her hearts desire. Eight of hearts or Water into Wine indicates a transformation of her current situation as well as the transformation or miracle of life occurring inside her womb.

2. Five of clubs or Crossroads in the middle indicates that the theme of this reading is about moving or going out onto the crossroads. Nine of diamonds or Mercury is also a traveling card and here may represent the vehicle or actual moving van. Mercury also represents business and

commerce and this move is for a new job. The fact that two out of the three cards cast are diamonds is a good sign for a job question. Eight of diamonds or Cornucopia in the outcome position indicates that the move will be a great success for him. Mirroring Mercury and Cornucopia indicates that by moving he will enjoy a period of great abundance by choosing to take the job and relocate.

3. Seven of clubs or Cross recognizes both the burden and stress of his prolonged unemployment and also is a work or labor card in itself. Four of diamonds or Cornerstone as the theme indicates work and his financial foundation. Four of clubs of Four Leaf Clover as the outcome card indicates that luck is coming and will sprout out of the seeds already planted. The Four Leaf Clover sprouts quickly and does not last forever indicating this opportunity that is coming is short lived and he must be ready to jump on the opportunity when it appears. Two fours here confirm that this issue is very important to his foundation in life. This short term luck if taken advantage of may affect his foundation long term and have lasting benefits. Another expression of the transitive nature of the Four Leaf Clover may be that this job opportunity may be only a temporary position with a definite end date or this position may lead to something better and more permanent. If the seven of diamonds or Finger of God appeared here, this would be a much stronger indication of luck and good fortune or the ace of diamonds or Sun card would also indicate a more enduring blessing.

Chapter 6

COMPLETION, JUVENILES AND YIN
TEN, JACK AND QUEEN

THE TEN. Ten is the card of completion. Ten reduced becomes one again. Here the hard work, the sweat and toil, victory or failure is given a final evaluation; a thumbs up or thumbs down. At ten we arrive at our destination for better or worse. Ten is the completion, reaching the pinnacle and new beginnings.

TEN OF HEARTS
CUP OVERFLOWING

Write this meaning at the top of the corresponding card in your practice deck.

The symbol of the ten of hearts is Cup Overflowing. The ten of cups represents a full heart, joy and love overflowing. Abundant blessings appear with this card. Ten is completion and fullness. The hearts suit indicates emotion, love, passion and the spirit.

Cup Overflowing in a reading may also represent being filled to overflowing with love, joy, happiness, peace, contentment, filled with the Holy Spirit, unconditional love, feeling loved, blessings given and received, charity, giving from the abundance of your heart, gay and a bubbly personality.

TEN OF DIAMONDS
INHERITANCE

Write this meaning at the top of the corresponding card in your practice deck.

The symbol of the ten of diamonds is Inheritance. Upon the passing of a close relative or loved one, property and title are passed to the heirs. An Inheritance happens suddenly, usually unexpectedly and often without accounting for either the positive or negative actions of the heir. Inheritance is a result of a life-long relationship and this relationship has gone through countless ups and downs, trials and tribulations, victories small and large. Inheritance takes a long time to arrive and is not easily lost.

Inheritance in a reading represents success, financial security, legacy, privilege, retirement, a well earned reward after a long and difficult journey, completion, family support, accomplishment and wealth.

TEN OF CLUBS
HAMSTER WHEEL

Write this meaning at the top of the corresponding card in your practice deck.

The symbol of the ten of clubs is the Hamster Wheel. The Hamster runs on his wheel. Whether he runs fast or slow or decides to sleep, take a personal day or call in sick to ignore the wheel, the wheel exists as a permanent fixture and he never seems to get anywhere. The Hamster Wheel represents the daily grind of life. Two steps forward and three steps back. Every day we, the hamsters, get up and go to our jobs and run on the Hamster Wheel. We get in our cars and drive and drive in the endless traffic; we pick up the kids; we buy groceries; we go to work; we go home; we pay bills; we get up and do it again; this is the Hamster Wheel.

Hamster Wheel in a reading represents the rat race, the business of life, the countless mundane details of daily existence, the daily grind, treading water, the never ending "to do" list, the journey of life, commuting, a long trip, traveling over water, international locations, long distances, running a marathon, and long term goals.

TEN OF SPADES
EARTHQUAKE

Write this meaning at the top of the corresponding card in your practice deck.

The symbol of the ten of spades is Earthquake. When the Earthquake card appears a violent shake up will ensue and something will come to a sudden and violent end. The seekers world is rocked to its very foundations. The seeker may have invested weeks, months, years or even a life time building upon this financial, relational or material foundation only to see it come crashing down very suddenly.

Ten represents completion and spades represent conflict and energy that reverses upon itself and becomes destructive.

Earthquake in a reading represents the ending of a way of life; financial ruin; the end of a long term relationship; a violent or disastrous ending; sudden downfall; defeat; misfortune; betrayal; crash or a serious accident. The spades suit also indicates the mind and in a reading may also represent a nightmare; insanity; rock bottom; or the seekers darkest hour.

MULTIPLE TENS APPEARING IN A READING

Ten represents completion and success; fullness of joy; wealth and inheritance; a long journey and the violent sweeping away of old foundations.

Four tens appearing together in a reading indicates rejecting what is inferior and outdated to embrace what is superior. The rejection of the old leads to immediate success and a dream come true.

Three tens and two tens in a reading respectively indicate reaching the mountain top of completion and success in the area's represented. Ten of spades or Earthquake also represents completion but in the sense of failure or the destruction of the intended goal. The ten is very much like a final verdict for the situation represented. A new cycle will begin shortly following the appearance of the ten.

THE JACK- The jack indicates a new beginning. The jack can be male or female. The jack represents someone who is not yet set in his/her ways, an immature, youthful, flexible and opportunistic person in action or thought. Age is not a factor and a jack in a reading can be young person, an old person or anywhere in between.

In the card numbering system, the jack is the eleventh card or ten plus one. Therefore, a jack in addition to representing a person also represents a fresh start and a new beginning, fresh thinking and opportunity grasped.

JACK OF HEARTS
ANGEL

Write this meaning at the top of the corresponding card in your practice deck.

The symbol of the jack of hearts is the Angel. The Angel represents a person in a situation that is trustworthy, generous, compassionate, kind and helpful. They may also be very unselfish, giving, loving, happy and reliable. The Angel is exactly who the seeker can rely upon and lean on in the midst of the challenges and difficulties of life.

The Angel card may represent a literal angel. Alternatively, this card may reveal a person who is only "acting" like an angel but the other cards present may reveal the presence of negative ulterior motives. Belonging to the hearts suit, the Angel represents more about love, spirituality and purity of intention than it represents concrete actions.

The Angel in a reading is someone who carries no emotional baggage into the situation. They are innocent, generous, trustworthy, child like, truthful, pure of heart and intention, good, spiritual, compassionate and the favorite son or daughter.

JACK OF DIAMONDS
PLAYER

Write this meaning at the top of the corresponding card in your practice deck.

The symbol of the jack of diamonds is the Player. The Player is a risk taker, smooth talker, attractive and persuasive. The Player, like all the jacks, can be either male or female. The jack is a juvenile, so the energy is new and very fresh. The Player may represent someone the seeker meets in a nightclub, at the gaming tables in Vegas, starting a new job or in the produce department at the grocery. The Player is full of optimism, has some cash to spend, new clothes, and is not yet burdened by the troubles of life. The Player corresponds closely to the fool card of the tarot.

The Player in a reading represents a new situation, a fresh start, the new guy or gal, a sharp dresser, glib talker, handsome, attractive, flashy, witty, sociable, a young lawyer, business person or the beginning of a successful new venture or relationship. The Player is full of energy, optimism and zest for life.

JACK OF CLUBS
STRENGTH

Write this meaning at the top of the corresponding card in your practice deck.

The symbol of the jack of clubs is Strength. I once went on my favorite local hike with my muscle bound friend visiting from the other coast. The hike was ten miles total with an elevation change of fifteen hundred feet each way. Within two miles, he was gasping for breath, jokingly accusing me of attempting to kill him and demanding frequently that we stop for water breaks of which I realized suddenly that he would surely run out of water before reaching the peak. I knew from experience that I would drink less than half the water I had brought. He had brought more than three times the amount of water as myself and had nearly consumed all of it a mere one quarter of the way into the hike. He was sweating profusely already and was boasting about how much water he regularly forced down his throat every day for health reasons. Standing side by side in a photo, no one would assume that the smaller, older man with the slight paunch was in better condition than the much larger man with the six pack abs and the fabulous muscles and confident smile who worked out religiously several hours a day at the gym.

I had several advantages over my friend. I had done that hike dozens of times before and I loved all of it. I loved the fresh air, the push before breaking the tree line, the elevation of my breath and the first sweat. After the first sweat, my breath and heart rate would drop dramatically to a very comfortable rhythm and I would catch my hiking stride. I knew when to push, where to stop and the best spots to sip some water and enjoy the views. Although I admit to having strong legs, a strong back and clear lungs, I did not have impressive muscles like my friend. Most, if not all of my advantages were internal.

Strength in a reading is about determination, self control, mastery, patience, courage, motivation, endurance, fortitude, long suffering, mind over matter and not giving up. Strength in a reading may also represent force, big, massive and aggressive.

JACK OF SPADES
DEVIL

Write this meaning at the top of the corresponding card in your practice deck.

The symbol of the jack of spades is the Devil. The Devil is a juvenile card and its nature is to enjoy the evil and destruction wrought in the moment without thought of future consequences. Like all jacks, the Devil card can equally represent a male or female in a reading.

The Devil is the personification of evil; a thief, a liar, an angry or malicious person, selfish, childish, bad intentioned, envious, lazy, jealous, covetous, self destructive or depraved. Not only will the Devil seek to directly harm the seeker, but will just as often try to lead them both together down a dangerous, self destructive path where they will harm themselves or others and become so entangled that they lose hope. Therefore, the Devil card also represents someone who lures the seeker into an elaborate trap in order to fulfill their own twisted desires related to alcohol, drugs, sex, sensuality, bondage, fleshly indulgence, excess, obsession, immediate gratification, pornography, demonic rituals, dark magic and dark occult rituals. The Devil represents a bad boy or girl, someone with dark secrets, a criminal, sadistic, mean, cruel, a sociopath, a psychopath, mister or misses Wrong, someone suffering from addiction, Satanist, evil person, a person with very dark energy, an abuser, demons and the literal Devil of the Bible.

MULTIPLE JACKS APPEARING IN A READING

Four jacks appearing together in a reading may indicate a very attractive new situation with a dangerous undercurrent or element.

Three jacks and two jacks in a reading respectively indicate an outing with new friends or new venues. The energy of the jack is young, flexible, optimistic and world shaking but does not have great endurance without other supporting cards. The seeker should be careful whenever the jack of spades appears as it is perhaps the most consistently negative energy represented by the cards.

THE QUEEN. The queen represents mature female energy or yin energy. Yin energy is passive, receptive, reactive, negative, restrictive, concealed, hidden, dark, and moon. The queen represents feelings, emotions, nurture, mothering and earth energy. The queen in a reading may represent a literal woman but equally as often the queen will represent the energy present in the situation and therefore the actions of either male or female participants.

QUEEN OF HEARTS
WOMAN

Write this meaning at the top of the corresponding card in your practice deck.

The symbol of the queen of hearts is the Woman. Represented by the hearts suit, the Woman card represents a neutral to positive adult female figure acting without any major ulterior motives or acting negatively in the spread, although other cards may indicate negative actions and forces directed against her. If the seeker is a female, then this card will often represent her in the reading. The Woman card may also represent a neutral to positive environment or situation.

The Woman in a reading represents an adult female who is friendly, trustworthy, nurturing, kind, loving, gentle, beloved, girl friend, friend, fiancé, wife, lover, significant other, sister, important female, feminine behavior, a Woman with no hidden agenda, having a pure heart and motivations.

QUEEN OF DIAMONDS
FOX

Write this meaning at the top of the corresponding card in your practice deck.

The symbol of the queen of diamonds is the Fox. The Fox represents someone who is cunning, deceptive and has selfish motives. The Fox plays elaborate games to win any advantage; she is clever, witty, attractive, manipulative and materialistic. The Fox may represent a business person who may be male or female as well as the conduct of any form of business. The Fox may also represent a well groomed, beautiful woman who navigates her world with confidence. The Fox is not necessarily female but feminine yin energy.

The queen corresponds to the number twelve or ten plus two. Ten represents completion and completed energy. The two is about union and partnerships. The queen is feminine energy and is dominated by the yin energy of the yin and yang. The diamond suit represents money and communication.

Fox in a reading may represent a someone who is manipulative, cunning, a trickster, con artist, crafty, independent, gold digger, materialistic, shrewd, untrustworthy, promoting a hidden agenda, treacherous, shifty, duplicitous, deceptive, deceitful, criminal, police detective, seductive, attractive, represent the other woman in an adulterous relationship and a male or female with red hair.

QUEEN OF CLUBS
MOTHER EARTH

Write this meaning at the top of the corresponding card in your practice deck.

The symbol of the queen of clubs is Mother Earth. Mother Earth represents pure earth energy and is a positive expression of nurturing feminine energy. This nurture usually represents the situation but may also be expressed equally by male or female persons within the situation.

Mother Earth represents fertility, pregnancy, reproduction, fruitfulness, femininity, beauty, spending time in nature, gardening, growth, creativity, sensuality, nurture, settling down, home maker, child care, domestic duties, safe and secure environment, happy home and a supportive community.

QUEEN OF SPADES
SNAKE

Write this meaning at the top of the corresponding card in your practice deck.

The symbol of the queen of spades is the Snake. A Snake in the wild will not usually be seen chasing an antelope across the African savanna; rather the Snake lays in wait for its victim. The Snake disguises itself as a tree branch or brush on the ground and waits for its victim to come to it. The Snake is infamous for its legendary deception of the first woman Eve in the Garden of Eden and the subsequent fall of human kind from God's grace.

The Snake is intelligent, crafty, ruthless, backstabbing, jealous, plotting, patient, vengeful and a betrayer of trust. The Snake disguises itself within the existing environment, manipulating the environment and those within it as well as any and all means at its disposal to accomplish its hidden goals including guilt, jealousy, extortion, other persons, events and violence.

The Snake in the Bible was considered to be among the most beautiful and intelligent of God's creatures on the earth. The Snake in a reading is attractive, sexy, sleek, slim, strong, athletic, the other woman, an adulterous woman, manipulative, deceptive, sends mixed messages, speaks with a forked tongue and intentionally creates confusion. The Snake may also represent Satan, Lucifer, dark magic, plumbing, a literal snake, intestines, bowels, an internal illness or disease, complications, an affair, an enemy and the medical caduceus.

The Snake in a reading may equally represent a male or female person or the situation itself.

MULTIPLE QUEENS APPEARING IN A READING

Four queens appearing together in a reading may indicate an overload of drama and conflict in a situation or among a group of people usually women. Beware of hidden traps.

Three queens and may indicate rivalry, jealousy or underhanded dealings.

Two queens may indicate two females interacting.

TEN SAMPLE CARD PAIRINGS ACE THROUGH QUEEN

We now have three more cards with which to work. Let's do ten sample card pairings using all twelve cards now available to us.

Ten of diamonds and nine of diamonds = Inheritance and Mercury. A will or inheritance coming; a college diploma; a winning lottery ticket.

Ten of clubs and six of clubs = Hamster Wheel and Olive Tree. A trip to see family; handling endless daily family affairs and chores; the daily grind of living.

Ten of spades and four of diamonds = Earthquake and Cornerstone. Bankruptcy; house foreclosure; financial disaster.

Jack of spades and seven of clubs = Devil and Cross. Feeling trapped in a very difficult or impossible situation; an evil person intends the seeker harm; temptation.

Jack of hearts and three of clubs = Angel and Three Black Birds. Prayers to God; talking to close friends or family having the seekers best interest in mind; answer to prayer.

Jack of diamonds and four of clubs = Player and Four Leaf Clover. A bit of gambling luck; getting lucky in love; the seekers lucky day.

Queen of clubs and three of hearts = Mother Earth and Roses. Pregnancy; a Mother's Day gift; party for mother; tending to the roses in the garden; enjoying a lovely day outside.

Queen of diamonds and two of diamonds = Fox and Diamond Ring. A business person executes a contract; a single woman accepts a date; an engagement.

Queen of hearts and jack of diamonds = Woman and Player. Woman meets a new man; blind date; Woman meets a man who is a bit of a player or ladies man; Woman begins a new situation.

Queen of spades and six of diamonds = Snake and Hand in Hand. Tares among the wheat; someone appears to be working in cooperation with others but is working for their own purposes; hidden criminal activities.

THREE CARD SPREADS

Here are some sample three card spreads using the cards ace to queen. Try unpacking these three spreads by your self before reading the answers below.

1. A woman asks, "Is my husband unfaithful?" She casts three of spades, three of hearts and queen of spades = Scourge, Roses and Snake.

2. A man asks, "I'm beginning a job in a completely new industry. How will it go?" He casts jack of diamonds, queen of clubs and ace of hearts = Player, Mother Earth and Heart.

3. A man is taking classes in night school. He asks, "Will I finally graduate this year?" He casts four of clubs, ace of clubs and ten of diamonds = Four Leaf Clover, Mustard Seed and Inheritance.

SAMPLE ANSWERS

1. Is her husband unfaithful? Three is a crowd and there are two threes are present in this small spread. Three of spades or Scourge is first. Scourge represents a repeated conflict and something chipping away at the foundation of their marriage. Three of hearts or Roses is next. The Roses card represents something sweet, romance or a woman's vagina. Roses carry a most feminine energy. The final card is the queen of spades or Snake. The Snake card represents an adulterous woman here. The husband is relentlessly chipping away at the foundation of the marriage (Scourge) by having adulterous affairs with other women (Snake) for the sweet romantic enjoyment of sex (Roses). At least there are no love cards present in this spread. Without further investigation here, it seems that these are just

romantic flings and not love relationships. However, they are definitely damaging to the foundation of the marriage.

2. How will it go in his new job? He's going to love his new job. Player is the seeker taking a risk and starting this new job. The Player is full of optimism, energy and zest for life and therefore the Player card corresponds closely to the fool of tarot. Mother Earth indicates that the environment is excellent for long term growth and nurturance of his career goals. Heart in the outcome position indicates he will be very happy there and he will love his new job and career field.

3. Will he finally graduate or burn out? Inheritance as outcome indicates success and accomplishment of a long term goal. The Four Leaf Clover is short term luck or an opportunity that requires continued effort and activity on his part. The Four Leaf Clover is a very active, earthy grounded card and can also represent exercising. Mustard Seed represents the literal diploma and the start of something new that has the ability to grow into something very big. He will achieve his graduation goal and this will be the beginning of very big and positive changes in his life.

Chapter 7

YANG ENERGY, TRANSFORMATION AND DESTINY
KING, RED JOKER & BLUE JOKER

THE KING. Just as the queen represents mature female energy, the king represents mature male energy. The king in a reading may represent a literal man but very frequently represents the energy present in the situation. The king represents directed action, aggression, change, and the focused exertion of the human will.

KING OF HEARTS
MAN

Write this meaning at the top of the corresponding card in your practice deck.

The symbol of the king of hearts is the Man. The Man card in readings represents a neutral to positive adult male figure. Represented by the heart suit, he is a positive person without any major ulterior motives or acting negatively in the spread, although other cards may indicate negative actions and forces directed against him. If the seeker is a male, then this card will usually represent him in the reading. If the seeker's question concerns a male, then this card will usually represent him.

The Man in a reading may represent the seeker, a mature male, friendly, trustworthy, kind, loving, gentle, beloved, boy friend, husband, lover, romantic partner, fiancé, significant other, important male, friend, masculine energy, trust worthy, no hidden agenda, having a pure heart and motivations.

KING OF DIAMONDS
MAGI

Write this meaning at the top of the corresponding card in your practice deck.

The symbol of the king of diamonds is the Magi. Since this fortune telling method is called the "Magi Method" the story of the three wise men bears repeating. The three Magi of the Bible also known as the three kings and the three wise men were present at the birth of Jesus the Christ in Bethlehem in a cattle stall and brought gold, frankincense and myrrh to celebrate this most auspicious birth. According to the Magi themselves, they learned of this birth through astrology or the movements of the celestial bodies interpreted spiritually and applied to human events. Further, these Magi interpreted long lost extra-biblical scrolls and prophecies foretelling the birth of the Christ. On the basis of astrology and these prophecies, they undertook a long and perilous journey to be present at this birth. It is worth noting that the only luminaries present at the birth of Jesus were these three Magi. There were no high priests or Levites present nor were there any kings or high officials of any court, only Joseph and Mary, these three Magi, a few illiterate shepherds, some livestock and some angels of God attended.

In those days, there was no separation of church and state. In fact, every king and queen believed they were of divine origin; a literal god or goddess. Therefore, kings surrounded themselves with others who demonstrated a connection to the divine. These persons were called Magi. Magi were among the most powerful persons on earth and sometimes wielded even more power than the king. Magi sat on the high counsel of advisors to the king and acted as governors and administrators of the king's decrees. A good example of this is Daniel the prophet who was appointed by king Nebuchadnezzar of Babylon as "chief of the magicians, enchanters, astrologers and diviners." Daniel 5:11. King Nebuchadnezzar was perhaps the most powerful man on earth in his day. The prophet Daniel was famous for his devotion to God which resulted in his being thrown into the lion's den to be torn apart by hungry ferocious beasts and also resulted in his being thrown into the fiery furnace to be burned alive.

All decisions went before the king's high counsel before presentation to the king. Daniel was the chief cabinet minister and the highest governing official after the king. Each important decision was considered using various forms of divination to seek divine guidance as well as the usual methods employed today. In other words, Daniel the prophet of God typically performed dozens of divinations on a daily basis as well as astrology, magic (binding and loosing) and enchantment. This was his job. Magi were so learned and wise; so powerful and highly esteemed that they were commonly extended the same honors as the king himself as we see in the biblical account of the Magi at the birth of the Christ.

The Magi in a reading represents personal power, authority, focus, determination, magic, commanding the spirits, exorcist, will, manifestation of desires, can do attitude, wisdom, knowledge, prophecy, dream interpretation, foresight, critical thinking, good communication skills, business person and success.

KING OF CLUBS
RULER

Write this meaning at the top of the corresponding card in your practice deck.

The symbol of the king of clubs is the Ruler. Just as Mother Earth is the feminine principle, Ruler is the masculine principle operating in the world. Everyone answers to someone and that person is the Ruler. The Ruler creates, maintains and thrives on structure. The Ruler may be a politician, government official, manager, boss, head of household, president of the home owners association, police force, police officer or father.

The Ruler in readings represents structure, authority and dominance. The Ruler is fatherly, practical, stable, worldly, protector, provider, patriarch, rules, regulations and government, authoritative and powerful.

KING OF SPADES
EXECUTIONER

Write this meaning at the top of the corresponding card in your practice deck.

The symbol of the king of spades is the Executioner. The Executioner wears a black hooded mask so that he may remain nameless and faceless. He wears black clothing and carries a two edged sword with a long handle. The Executioner has authority not because of who he or she is but because of who they represent as part of a larger organization. The Executioner takes without asking and no one can stop them. The Executioner has the authority, justly or unjustly, to do whatever they may decide on the spot. The Executioner always acts without feeling on principle, position and the concept that might is always right.

The energy of the Executioner is different than the Devil card. The Devil or jack of spades is a juvenile and as such may harm the seeker and others out of simple malice, unrestrained emotion or anger. The energy of the Executioner is a much more mature, focused and directed energy and may have a much greater impact with less effort. The Executioner has the power to harm or heal.

The Executioner in readings represents a judge, judgment, a police officer, probation officer, corrections officer, doctor, lawyer, criminal organization, mob boss, murderer, thief, prince of demons or anyone or any organization large and powerful enough that they cannot be resisted by the seeker alone. The Executioner may also represent someone who is very depressed, very serious or demonstrates very dark energy.

MULTIPLE KINGS APPEARING IN A READING

Although the energy of the kings is very male, yang energy, any of the court cards may represent a male or female person acting with this energy. In other words, the kings' appearance in a reading may often or even usually represent a literal male, but may also represent one or more literal female persons acting with this energy. The same applies to the queens and jacks. None of the trumps are literally male or female, but rather male or female yang or yin dominated energies.

Four kings appearing together in a reading may indicate ascending to or holding a powerful public position recognized by many.

Three kings and two kings respectively emphasize authority, dominance and mastery either by the seeker or against the seeker in the area indicated by the question and the other cards.

THE JOKER. The Joker is a card of transformation, renewal, opportunity, major turning points and karmic shift. The energy of the red joker is very light and fleeting while the energy of the blue joker is stronger, deeper and longer lasting.

RED JOKER
BUTTERFLY

Write this meaning at the top of the corresponding card in your practice deck.

The symbol of the red joker is the Butterfly. The Butterfly begins its life cycle as a destructive, eating machine in the form of an ugly, gluttonous caterpillar. At the end of this cycle of unbridled gluttony and destruction, the caterpillar spins itself into a cocoon or chrysalis. Inside the chrysalis, the caterpillar transforms and remerges as the beautiful butterfly.

The Butterfly in a reading represents renewal, transformation, beauty, freedom, a fresh start, new, popular, outgoing, social butterfly, limited attention span, sex and attraction.

The Butterfly in a reading acts quickly to bring change, but this opportunity for change may pass quickly if not acted upon.

BLUE JOKER
KARMIC SHIFT

Write this meaning at the top of the corresponding card in your practice deck.

The symbol of the blue joker is the Karmic Shift. The Karmic Shift in readings represents a major change. The rules have suddenly changed; suddenly an opportunity opens that was previously closed and seemed lost or an opportunity appears that was never previously imagined. Karmic Shift is about the larger strokes of destiny shaping the seekers life here on earth and the divine reasons for traveling this path.

The Karmic Shift in readings represents karma, fate, a major shift in perspective, major life change, big opportunity, events occurring beneath the surface of the seekers awareness that may change everything, turning point, paradigm shift, fundamental change in situation, foreordained and destiny.

MULTIPLE JOKERS APPEARING IN A READING

Both jokers appearing in a reading indicates change that will occur immediately and has the power to transform the situation and circumstances long term and even permanently. God gave us free will, however, and these opportunities must be grasped and acted upon or they may pass away to bear no fruit in the life of the seeker.

TEN SAMPLE CARD PAIRINGS ACE THROUGH JOKER

We now have complete card meanings for *all* fifty four cards. When I was a teen, my friend and I used to cruise the town in his car. He would suddenly yell dance break! We would jump out of the car and dance for a few minutes wherever we might find ourselves, whether at a traffic light, in the fast food drive through or in a parking lot. After a long journey together, we have finished all of the meanings of the fifty four cards. I decree a celebratory dance break; wherever you are - whether you are male or female, age nine to ninety or anywhere in between; stop, pop and break it down. Dance break!

Let's do some sample card pairings using all of the cards now available to us.

King of hearts and jack of diamonds = Man and Player. Man running his game in the dating world; Man has a fresh new start in life; Man born again.

King of diamonds and eight of spades = Magi and Scapegoat. Business man loses his job; business man diagnosed with a serious illness; business man loses his reputation.

King of spades and nine of clubs = Executioner and High Tower. Judge sentences (man) to prison for crimes; criminal sentenced to prison; powerful government official; depressed man suffering from agoraphobia.

Four of spades and red joker = Coffin and Butterfly. An ending leads immediately to a new beginning; out with the old, in with the new; the phoenix rises from the ashes.

Red joker and six of hearts = Butterfly and Karmic Relationship. Rekindling a past relationship; forgiving a person who hurt the seeker in the past; reunited with a family member who was missing from the seekers life for a long time.

Blue joker and two of hearts = Karmic Shift and Lovers. Destined love; the one; this person will change your life; true love that will endure; finding a purpose in life.

Blue joker and ten of clubs = Karmic Shift and Hamster Wheel; a life changing opportunity; extended travel that will change the seekers life; a radical change in the seekers life path.

Five of hearts and red joker = Fence Sitter and Butterfly. Undecided regarding a life changing decision; a life change already occurring in the spiritual realm as yet unrealized in this physical world; endlessly changing their mind for no apparent reason; flirting.

THREE CARD SPREADS

Here are some sample three card spreads using all of the cards. Try unpacking these three spreads on your own before reading the answers below.

1. A man asks, "Will I get the promotion at work?" He casts two of diamonds, jack of diamonds and six of diamonds = Ring, Player and Hand in Hand.

2. A man asks, "If I buy an investment property with Andy, how will it turn out?" He casts king of diamonds, four of diamonds and ten of spades = Magi, Cornerstone and Earthquake.

3. A woman sees her high school sweet heart after ten years apart. They have coffee and find out they are both now single. They exchange phone numbers. She asks, "It's been a long time. Should I take a chance on him?" She casts the blue joker, six of hearts and ace of hearts = Karmic Shift, Karmic Relationship and Heart.

SAMPLE ANSWERS

1. Will he get the promotion at work? Ring says union and contract. Player is a new situation and the person in a new situation. Hand in Hand indicates people working together toward the same goals. Yes, he will get this promotion.

2. How will the investment with Andy turn out? The Magi card indicates he has the funds and the ability to get this investment done. Cornerstone in the center is the literal house or four walls and foundation. Earthquake indicates that this investment will be a personal disaster. There's not enough cards here to indicate why this might

be a disaster and I would encourage the seeker to cast more cards with different related questions to learn more.

3. It seems to be going well so far. Should she take a chance on her old sweetheart? Karmic Relationship in the center indicates that she and this man have both a history and a deep connection, perhaps a soul connection. Let's see. Karmic Shift indicates that this relationship can completely change the current direction of her life. Heart at the end indicates real feeling present. She should go for it.

Chapter 8

DEDICATING AND CLEARING YOUR CARDS

Now that all your cards have meanings, you must dedicate your cards to God. As previously stated, the secrets of divination were reserved for kings and high priests. The urim and thummim of the biblical Old Testament were detachable stones designed specifically for divination and worn by the Hebrew high priest according to God's command. It is also taught that a person is not qualified to study kabala before the age of forty. The primary reason for the strict limitation of this knowledge is the fact that fortune telling and the art and science of divination are extremely powerful and therefore may be very dangerous to someone unprepared for entrance into this unseen world.

The proper dedication and clearing of your cards of unwelcome, base spirits is essential to obtaining good advice. If you read with cards that are not cleared of unclean spirits, the advice received will not be for your highest good and may lead you astray.

Fortune telling and divination are the processes by which we obtain the guidance of the divine and unseen forces beyond our physical plane. Many spirits both clean and craven, those that serve God above and those that are opposed to God are eager to connect to our physical world through the mundane instrument of playing card divination. It is absolutely essential, therefore, that we define whom we will welcome to speak to us during any casting of the cards.

In any working with the unseen world of the divine, we never communicate on an open channel. Always, we define the boundaries by intentionally giving permission to those spirits with whom we willingly communicate and we banish and bind any unwelcome spirits.

The first step is recognizing that you as a human being made in the image of God have the authority to command the spirits. Many passages in the Bible describe this fact. One of my favorites is in the gospel according to Matthew, chapter 16, verse 19 "I give you the keys to the kingdom of heaven; whatsoever you bind on the earth shall be bound in heaven and whatsoever you loose on this earth shall be loosed in heaven."

FIRST METHOD FOR CLEARING YOUR CARDS

1. Hold your dominant hand (the right hand if you are right handed) over your practice deck and your seekers deck and say the following, "I bind and banish all unclean spirits that seek to speak through these cards. I dedicate these cards to the purposes of God and His truth."

2. Pray Psalm 23 over your cards. I like Psalm 23 because the topic is God's help on our walk through this world which is the purpose behind divining with cards.

The Lord is my shepherd, I shall not want.
He makes me lie down in green pastures,
he leads me beside quiet waters,
he restores my soul.
He guides me in the paths of righteousness
for his name's sake.
Even though I walk
through the valley of the shadow of death,
I will fear no evil,
for you are with me;
your rod and your staff,
they comfort me.
You prepare a table before me
in the presence of my enemies.
You anoint my head with oil;
my cup overflows.
Surely your goodness and love will follow me
all the days of my life,
and I will dwell in the house of the Lord
forever.

3. Anoint the box containing the cards lightly with a dab of holy water. You may obtain holy water from a local Catholic Shrine or church.

4. Shuffle your cards and cast a three card spread asking:

        a. Whom do you serve?

        b. Do you love God?

You may also command them saying:

        c. Adore thy creator.

        d. Love the Lord your God with all your heart, mind, soul and strength.

I recommend casting only three cards for these questions. The cards *will not lie* to you as there are rules governing these things. They will clearly answer your questions. However, if they clearly tell you whom they serve and you don't like the answer and you ask them ten or twenty more times in one day, they may begin to give evasive or deceptive answers to appear to give you the answer you want especially if your follow up questions are not as clear as your initial questions. Your behavior has effectively given them permission.

This is a process. Sometimes the cards will obey me immediately and sometimes I have to let them sit for as long as nine days before they will finally read according to my commands. During this period of cleansing the cards, I read with my other clean decks and every day I will pick up the new decks and repeat the process outlined above and ask them some very direct questions. Once the spirits realize that you mean what you say, they obey and they maintain this state with very little maintenance.

SECOND METHOD FOR CLEARING YOUR CARDS

1. Smudge your cards with sage by passing them through sage smoke while praying over them.

2. Wrap them in a plastic sandwich bag and give them a salt bath in direct sunlight for three days. All of these procedures may be effective and act together for the same results.

3. Other Psalms and prayers may be employed in lieu of or in addition to Psalm 23 such as the prayer to "Our Father" and the prayer to St. Michael the Archangel.

The "Our Father" prayer is taught in the gospel of Matthew chapter six, verses nine through thirteen.

The Prayer to St. Michael the Archangel:

St. Michael the Archangel,
Defend us in battle
Be our protection against
The malice and snares of the devil.
May God rebuke him we humbly pray.
Michael, prince of the heavenly host,
By the power of God
Cast into hell Satan
And all evil spirits
Who roam the earth
Seeking the destruction of men's souls.
Amen.

ADDITIONAL SUGGESTIONS FOR KEEPING YOUR CARDS CLEAR OF UNWELCOME SPIRITS

1. My decks sit beneath the 72 names of God written in Hebrew when not in use.

2. You may set over where you store your cards one of the seals of the mighty Archangels Michael or Raphael.

3. Cast a circle and dedicate your cards to God using the four elements and cardinal directions. Call upon the names of God and the specific energies you wish to divine through your cards. I work regularly with the Archangels Michael, Raphael, Gabriel and Ariel. Mother Mary is particularly strong, kind and nurturing. Casting a circle is a more advanced work and I do not recommend this technique for a beginner unless you already have some knowledge of protection techniques and commanding the spirits.

Chapter 9

TECHNIQUES EMPLOYING 3, 5 AND 7 CARD SPREADS

WORKING WITH SPREADS

Entire books are written on fortune telling card spreads so my purpose here is to share a few of my favorite spreads that I frequently use. Typically, fortune tellers find a few spreads that speak clearly to them and they stick with those spreads.

JOURNALING - I recommend that you purchase a journal to write down your questions, cards cast and your interpretation of these cards and any follow up insights later. This is the fastest way to learn the cards and their relationships and meanings. I also recommend taking a photo of your casts and emailing it to yourself with an interpretation of the cards. I do not recommend keeping only electronic records in lieu of a written journal. I find the act of writing to be an important element of learning and processing the advice provided by the cards.

CARD PAIRINGS - The first and most basic spreading technique is card pairings. The relationships between the cards are very important and cards should be read in relation to the other cards around them and in relationship to the question. Card pairing is the most important technique to learning to read proficiently

HOW TO READ THE 3 CARD SPREAD

The three card spread is officially a position-less spread and as a result is very free flowing. Shuffle your cards while thinking about your question and cast three cards in a line.

CARD 1/ CARD 2/ CARD 3

I recommend that you cast at least one three card spread a day until you gain a basic familiarity with the meanings of all of your cards and their relationships to each other. The three card spread is the quickest and easiest way to get a clear answer to a question. Always ask a clear question and write it down before shuffling and casting the cards.

CARD 1 - represents the past and events leading up to the current state of affairs.

CARD 2 – represents the present. This card usually illuminates the current situation and the heart of the matter. This card will also often illuminate the emotional state of the seeker and their thoughts and feelings affecting the core of the question. In any odd numbered casting of cards 3, 5, 7 or 9 cards, the middle card in any reading also represents the theme of the reading.

CARD 3 – represents the future and the outcome of this situation. Card 3 also may represent the advice.

HOW TO READ THE 5 CARD AND 7 CARD SPREAD

Five card and seven card spreads are longer versions of three card spreads. You will find yourself very naturally casting longer spreads as you become more comfortable with your cards and their meanings. Shuffle your cards while stating your question out loud and cast five cards in a line like this:

CARD 1/ CARD 2/ CARD 3/ CARD 4/ CARD 5

You may have noticed that I am choosing to cast an odd number of cards each time. The reason for this is that CARD 3, the odd card or the middle card in a casting of any number of cards represents the theme of the reading.

CARD 1 and **CARD 2** – now represent the past and events leading up to the current state of affairs. We have simply added more information to the shorter three card spread.

CARD 3 – represents the theme and illuminates the thoughts and feelings of the seeker affecting the present situation.

CARD 4 and **CARD 5** – now gives more information on the future outcome of the situation as well as advice. Read the cards in pairs.

The seven card spread is laid in a line like this:

CARD 1/ CARD 2/ CARD 3/ CARD 4/ CARD 5/ CARD 6/ CARD 7

CARDS 1 to 3 – now represent the past and events leading to the current state of affairs.

CARDS 5 to 7 – represent the future, the outcome and advice.

CARD 4 – represents the theme and illuminates the present situation.

MIRRORING, COUNTING AND THE SHADOW CARD - ADDITIONAL TECHNIQUES WITH THE 3, 5 AND 7 CARD SPREAD

MIRRORING – This technique may be used with any three, five or seven card position-less spread.

CARD 1/ CARD 2/ CARD 3
CARD 1/ CARD 2/ CARD 3/ CARD 4/ CARD 5
CARD 1/ CARD 2/ CARD 3/ CARD 4/ CARD 5/ CARD 6/CARD7

Mirroring in a three card spread is accomplished by pairing **CARD 1** and **CARD 3** above or mirroring them to get extra meaning and guidance out of the spread. Because we threw an odd number of cards - three, five or seven in each spread, the middle card has no natural mirror.

In a five card spread therefore, **CARD 1** mirrors **CARD 5** and **CARD 2** mirrors **CARD 4**.

In a seven card spread **CARD 1** mirrors **CARD 7** and **CARD 2** mirrors **CARD 6** and **CARD 3** mirrors **CARD 5**.

COUNTING – The playing cards ace through ten are numbered literally as one through ten with the ace representing one. Jacks count as eleven. Queens count as twelve and kings count as thirteen

ACE = 1
TWO = 2
THREE = 3
FOUR = 4
FIVE = 5
SIX = 6
SEVEN = 7
EIGHT = 8
NINE = 9
TEN = 10
JACK = 11
QUEEN = 12
KING = 13

SHADOW CARD – The Shadow is the card appearing on the bottom of the deck after casting your spread. The Shadow Card is read as the hidden or unconscious reality beneath the cast. Many readers equate the Shadow Card to the crossing card or "what crosses the seeker" in the Celtic cross spread. It is added as a supplemental theme card in the reading for additional insight.

EXAMPLE USING 3 CARDS – Janet asks, "Will I get a new job soon?" She casts the jack of spades, ten of diamonds and two of diamonds = Devil, Inheritance and Diamond Ring. The shadow card appearing on the bottom of the deck after the shuffle is the four of clubs or Four Leaf Clover.

Let's start with some background on this cast. Janet, the seeker, tells me she quit her previous job a few months ago after a conflict with her supervisor during her regular performance review where he noted some areas of improvement that he wanted her to incorporate. This came as a shock to her and after a lot of subsequent discussion with her boss and other coworkers, she tendered her resignation. Janet has been unemployed since that time and is beginning to feel a little desperate financially as the bills keep piling up.

Devil in the past position indicates she was feeling trapped in a bad situation. The Devil is also a very bad person and often acts alone without consulting anyone else. Inheritance comes next in the present position. Inheritance is an excellent card in this position as it is a ten and a diamond. Diamonds are money and finances and the number ten indicates success and completion. The outcome card is Diamond Ring. Diamond Ring as the number two indicates a future union or a contract and in this case indicates Janet will soon begin a new job.

MIRRORING - we may mirror Devil and Diamond Ring to give us more information. Devil mirroring Diamond Ring reads as a very bad situation related to a contract, or in this case, at work. Devil is in the past so her last job was exceptionally bad or someone was even targeting her very personally. Devil mirroring Diamond Ring also indicates perhaps she was actually fired, laid off or let go from her previous job and may not be telling me due to feelings of embarrassment.

COUNTING - Janet asks the question, "Will I get a new job soon?" and cast the jack of spades, ten of diamonds and two of diamonds – Devil, Inheritance and Diamond Ring. We simply add up the cards. Jack of spades = 11. Ten of diamonds = 10. Two of diamonds = 2. 11+10+2= 23. The twenty third card in the deck is six of clubs or Olive Tree. We get this result by noting that there are four cards in each suit beginning with the ace and ending with the king. We count by fours. We count as the first card of each number hearts, then diamonds, then clubs and finally spades. The ace of hearts through the ace of spades counts to four; the two of hearts to the two of spades counts to eight. The twenty fourth card is the six of spades and the twenty second card is the six of diamonds. You may also write a number on each card of your practice deck beginning with the ace of hearts as #1 and ending with the blue joker as #54. The cards are numbered one through fifty four in order of appearance in this book. Please note that we only added the three original cards cast. We did not add the shadow card.

So in our example with Janet, "Will she get a new Job soon?" She cast Devil, Inheritance and Diamond Ring. We sum these cards to 23 and add the six of clubs = Olive Tree which we place directly above the ten of diamonds or

Inheritance. We read Inheritance and Olive Tree together in this instance as a confirmation that Janet will soon have success (Inheritance and Diamond Ring) in her job search and furthermore (Olive Tree) this is a job and a career field in which she can put down deep roots.

SHADOW CARD - The shadow card appearing on the bottom of the deck after the shuffle is the four of clubs or Four Leaf Clover. The Four Leaf Clover is placed directly below the ten of diamonds or Inheritance card. We read Four Leaf Clover and Inheritance together as good fortune successfully finding a good job and taking advantage of opportunities and activity that results in successfully obtaining a good job. We can further read together Four Leaf Clover, Inheritance and Olive Tree to read that a good job is gained through effort and luck that may last a very long time and lead to better things.

EXAMPLE USING 5 CARDS – Manuel asks, "Has my wife been unfaithful to me?" He casts king of diamonds, nine of spades, nine of clubs, six of hearts and four of diamonds = Magi, No, High Tower, Karmic Relationship, Cornerstone. The shadow card appearing on the bottom of the deck after the shuffle is the two of diamonds or Diamond Ring. The five cards cast add to 41 the jack of clubs or Strength.

The first thing that jumps out at me is that no female cards appear in this reading, but the Magi card or king of diamonds does appear. As previously noted, the kings do not necessarily represent a literal male, rather they represent male energy. Two other cards jump out at me which are the High Tower in the center and the No card in the second position. High Tower as theme indicates isolation, doing things by the book and safety. Isolation, being alone and doing things by the book doesn't look like an affair to me.

Next, in the past position we see the king of diamonds and nine of spades or Magi and No. The Magi is about manifestation of desires. I read the king of diamonds here as Manuel the seeker. The No card is a stop sign, feeling stuck or trapped. Manuel seems literally stuck on these thoughts that his wife may be having an affair. Again, High Tower in the center says, she has not been with anyone, but is instead alone.

In the future outcome position we have six of hearts and four of diamonds or Karmic Relationship and Cornerstone. Cornerstone represents the material foundation of the house including all of the physical things of this world. We have both High Tower and Cornerstone indicating a strong foundation present in this relationship.

Karmic Relationship pairs with Cornerstone giving us a very strong foundation both relationally with the six of hearts and materially with the four of diamonds.

MIRRORING - Now we mirror **CARD 1** and **CARD 5**, Magi and Cornerstone for more information. Manuel has the power to build on this solid foundation in his marriage. Next we mirror **CARD 2** and **CARD 4**, No and Karmic Relationship. This can be read, there is no other important relationship present and we can eliminate someone returning from her past.

A good practice is to ask yourself what cards you would expect to see if in fact Manuel's wife was being unfaithful. I would expect to see the queen of diamonds or Fox card. The Fox is very independent and selfish and often shows up in relationships related to cheating. I would also expect to see the six of spades or Incubus/Succubus card. The Incubus/Succubus represents a relationship that has gone toxic, unhealthy and may indicate some abuse. I would also expect to see the two of spades or Broken Chalice indicating a broken relationship between them. In relationship spreads we tend to see twos and sixes as well as male and female cards identifying key participants.

SHADOW CARD – Next we look at the two of diamonds or Diamond Ring which appeared as the shadow card. Two of diamonds pairs with the middle card the nine of clubs or Diamond Ring pairs with High Tower. These cards confirm that the marriage is strong and read that the marriage is literally going by the book or the marriage contract originally agreed.

COUNTING – Counting the original cast of five cards we arrive at 41 the jack of clubs or Strength. The jack of clubs pairs in the center with the nine of clubs and two of diamonds or Strength, High Tower and Diamond

Ring. A strong marriage and union is represented. Everything again is as it should be.

My advice to Manuel is to assure him that there is nothing in these cards to indicate his wife is cheating. Personally, I think that most of this is in his mind as indicated here by the Magi card and perhaps Manuel is having some jealousy issues. I also see nothing to indicate that Manuel is unfaithful and casting blame on his wife to hide his own illicit activities.

A seven card cast works the same as the five and three card cast with regard to mirroring, counting, shadow card and pairing.

Chapter 10

THE 9 CARD BOX SPREAD

THE BOX SPREAD

The nine card spread produces a more general reading of the circumstances surrounding the seeker. However, a clear and unambiguous question should be posed and written down before casting the nine cards for this oracle. The nine card spread is cast in a box shape like this:

CARD 1/ CARD 2/ CARD 3
CARD 4/ CARD 5/ CARD 6
CARD 7/ CARD 8/ CARD 9

Some cartomancers will also cast the nine card spread beginning with the center card and casting the spread in a clock wise, Fibonacci sequence. This is a matter of preference and I encourage the use of your growing intuition. Whichever order you prefer to cast the cards, the past present and future positions do not change in the spread.

CARD 5/ CARD 6/ CARD 7
CARD 4/ CARD 1/ CARD 8
CARD 3/ CARD 2/ CARD 9

In all of the following examples I will employ the first and simplest method of casting the nine cards to create the square of nine. There are manifold methods for unpacking the meanings in the box spread including getting an overall impression, reading the theme card, entrance and exit cards, past, present, future, knighting, mirroring, the inner diamond and the four corners for starters.

Frank asks, "Is it favorable for me to take the relocation with my company across the country?" He casts:

Three of spades/ two of clubs/ seven of clubs
King of clubs/ ten of clubs/ nine of clubs
Four of hearts/ queen of spades/ jack of clubs

These cards translate to:

Scourge/ Handcuffs/ Cross
Ruler/ Hamster Wheel/ High Tower
Home/ Snake/ Strength

Overall Impression- First is the overall impression. How does the spread look? Are there more black cards or red cards? Is there a lot of earth energy, money energy or water - hearts energy? My first and overall impression of this spread is that it is dark and heavy. It's all black suited cards except for the four of hearts or Home card. Also two spades appear which indicate conflict, problems and reversed energy. No diamonds appear in the spread to indicate money. I would definitely like to see diamonds in a work spread which will likely indicate prosperity. All the rest of the cards are clubs which are very solid, rooted energy. I'm not seeing a lot of happiness or joy in this move. This looks like a chore to me.

Center Card or Theme- First we read the center card which in this case is the ten of clubs meaning Hamster Wheel. This is a reading about work relocation, so this is not a bad card. However, just replacing this cast card with alternative potential tens, Frank could also have cast the ten of diamonds meaning Inheritance which would indicate this relocation would result in great success and more money or the ten of hearts meaning Cup Overflowing which would indicate that a very happy period of his life will result from this move. Hamster Wheel is not a happy or successful card but a card of burdens, drudgery and responsibility. Already, I'm not feeling excited about this move.

Entrance Card- Next we read the entrance card or **CARD 1** which is the three of spades meaning Scourge. The three of spades in a work context represents conflict that repeats, continues and festers. From the entrance we can see that if Frank takes this transfer he is walking into a conflict either probably at his new workplace or in his personal life related to this new job. Let's see what the other cards tell us.

Exit Card- **CARD 9** is the exit card and the jack of clubs meaning Strength. "What does not kill you makes you stronger" pops into my head on seeing this card. What kind of Strength this indicates will depend on the other cards surrounding it and relating to it. At this point, I feel Strength here is positive.

Past Rows-

CARD 1/ CARD 2/ CARD 3
CARD 4/
CARD 7/

CARD 1, 4 and **7** or **CARD 1, 2** and **3** may be read as the past or the circumstances leading up to the present situation. These cards also establish foundational issues that may be present in the situation.

Three of spades/ two of clubs/ seven of clubs
King of clubs/
Four of hearts/

Scourge/ Handcuffs/ Cross
Ruler/
Home/

Scourge, Handcuffs and Cross reads as conflict, joined to persons where there are no emotional feelings present as in a work environment and heavy burdens. Work here is not showing up as a family environment or a joyous place but a place of conflict and burdens and associations with persons for whom Frank has no personal feelings.

Down in the past row we read Scourge, Ruler and Home. These next three cards indicate festering problems at work in his relationships and possibly a conflict with his boss indicated by Scourge and Ruler. So, we can see that Frank's reason for considering this relocation is dissatisfaction with his work, the work environment and the relationship he has at his work with his boss. He seems to be hoping that this relocation will offer him an improved situation.

Present Rows-

CARD 2
CARD 4/ CARD 5/ CARD 6
CARD 8

Two of Clubs
King of clubs/ ten of clubs/ nine of clubs
Queen of spades

Handcuffs
Ruler/ Hamster Wheel/ High Tower
Snake

These two rows represent the present situation or events as they stand now in the situation about which the seeker is requesting information. In the present row proceeding down we read Handcuffs, Hamster Wheel and Snake. Frank's work is drudgery to him or as they say "same stuff, different day." The Handcuffs card indicates he doesn't feel any emotional connection to the people he works with and Snake indicates backstabbing, gossip and other negative entanglements at work. All in all, not a nice place to come to work every day.

Reading across we have Ruler, Hamster Wheel and High Tower. High Tower indicates he feels isolated and alone at work with no one to confide in. Ruler represents the work situation and probably his boss which he doesn't get along with swimmingly as indicated by Scourge and Ruler. We see that Frank really doesn't enjoy his work or the people there and he also feels that his co-workers gossip constantly as indicated by the Snake and are dangerous to his future at this work environment. As a result, he feels isolated and alone.

Future Rows-
CARD 3
CARD 6
CARD 7/ CARD 8/ CARD 9

Seven of clubs
Nine of clubs
Four of hearts/ queen of spades/jack of clubs

Cross
High Tower
Home/ Snake/ Strength

These two rows represent the future situation or events as they will most likely occur unless specific actions are taken by the seeker to avoid these future results. This future reading may be easily avoided by taking specific actions resulting in Frank choosing not to relocate with this job. In the future row proceeding down we read Cross, High Tower and Strength. Taking this path results in Frank feeling burdened and isolated in a new place far from familiar places and faces, but exits with Strength an interesting card. Across, the future row reads Home, Snake and Strength. Home here is new home and moving his home. Snake represents many complications and difficulties and Strength is probably personal growth as a result of the many hardships associated with Frank choosing this path. So if Frank is hoping to improve his work situation with this transfer, it doesn't look like any major improvement coming rather it appears that the burdens will continue and new complications will appear. On the bright side, the exit card is Strength which is about inner strength and self control. However, there is more we can learn from these individual cards by employing additional techniques.

Knighting- is a technique borrowed from chess. In the same way that a knight on a chess board moves one square up or down and two squares over and two squares up or down and one square over, we can read the relationships between the cards in a square of nine.

CARD 1/ CARD 2/ CARD 3
CARD 4/ CARD 5/ CARD 6
CARD 7/ CARD 8/ CARD 9

CARD 2
CARD 4
          CARD 9

Two of clubs
King of clubs
         Jack of clubs

Handcuffs
Ruler
         Strength

Let's begin by knighting the Strength card which appears as the last card in the future row in the exit position and therefore is a very important advice card. Above we see that **CARD 9** knights to **CARD 4** and **CARD 2** meaning the jack of clubs knights to the king of clubs and two of clubs or Strength knights to Ruler and Handcuffs. The Handcuffs is a card of union without emotion. Frank's character is strengthened by virtue of being surrounded by strangers in a new town and workplace and forced to work and live in a strange environment. Ruler is all about Frank taking charge of his environment. Also Ruler as previously suggested, may also be Frank's new boss. Frank's new environment will be very challenging to him personally and professionally and in order to survive, Frank will need to find his inner Napoleon and take charge of his life and environment. This results in positive changes for Frank.

We can actually knight from any card in the square of nine except the center card which cannot be knighted or mirrored. However, for learning purposes, we will knight a few cards including finally the seven of clubs or Cross card as another very interesting card. **CARD 3** knights **CARD 4** and **CARD 8**.

CARD 3
CARD 4
CARD 8

Seven of clubs

King of clubs

Queen of spades

Cross

Ruler

Snake

The Cross, like the cross of Jesus Christ, is a card of trial, suffering and heavy burdens. Reviewing the future row, we see Cross, High Tower and Strength meaning that heavy burdens and isolation make Frank Stronger. High

Tower may also mean that Frank will put in extra hours at work. By knighting to Cross we wish to find out more about the burdens represented here. The Cross knights to the queen of spades or Snake meaning that these heavy burdens are a result of complications at work, gossip from co-workers, as in an unfriendly, competitive and backstabbing environment or the Snake can often represent a woman. I would be curious to know if Frank will be working for a female supervisor in this new location and if so, I would expect this supervisor to cause Frank a lot of trouble. Cross also knights to Ruler. Ruler is usually a boss or person in authority. Now we see that Cross is knighting to both Ruler and Snake which greatly increases the probability that Frank's burdens at this new position will be increased by someone in authority over him and most likely this person will be a woman due to the appearance of the queen of spades or Snake card. This Snake may be a big boss or merely a team leader, but this person will surely exert authority over Frank.

We should knight one more card to get to the bottom of the supervisor and co-workers issue here. Let's knight the only red card appearing in this square of nine.

CARD 2
CARD 6
CARD 7

Two of clubs
Nine of clubs
Four of hearts

Handcuffs
High Tower

Home

We see the versatility of knighting here as we are knighting from the bottom upwards. **CARD 7** knights **CARD 6** and **CARD 2**. Here we begin with the four of hearts or Home card. Home indicates who Frank's friends will be in this new location. Who supports Frank and with whom does he feel comfortable? Home knights to High Tower and Handcuffs. The Handcuffs is a very impersonal card, so we know these are work relationships. The two of clubs tempers the emotions of the four of hearts and we read that Frank's new relationships with his coworkers are quite impersonal. Home also knights to High Tower indicating that Frank feels quite isolated at work. The queen of spades or Snake touches the four of hearts, nine of clubs and the king of clubs or the cards Home, High Tower and Ruler indicating that this Snake works closely with Frank (Snake and Home); isolates Frank at work (Snake and High Tower) and is likely in some managerial capacity over Frank (Snake and Ruler).

Inner Diamond- The inner diamond of the nine square represents the "inside scoop" on the situation or what's going on internally. The inner diamond is represented by the following card positions.

	CARD 2	
CARD 4		**CARD 6**
	CARD 8	

	Two of clubs	
King of clubs		Nine of clubs

Queen of spades

Handcuffs

Ruler   High Tower

Snake

I tend to read the inner diamond from the bottom card moving around in a clockwise fashion, but I have seen others read from the top moving clockwise and down. Here the inner diamond reads queen of spades, king of clubs, two of clubs and nine of clubs or Snake, Ruler, Handcuffs and High Tower. I interpret this as saying that a powerful, treacherous manager who is probably female (Snake and Ruler) is connected closely to Frank and causes him to feel very isolated at work (Handcuffs and High Tower). Basically, we've covered this ground already, but this technique shows that there's more than one way to arrive at the same conclusion in a square of nine. Also, employing additional techniques helps to add certainty and provide a sanity check of previous conclusions.

Mirroring and the four corners- are the final techniques we will employ here on this square of nine to squeeze as much wisdom and information out of this spread as possible.

CARD 1   **CARD 3**

CARD 7   **CARD 9**

Three of spades   seven of clubs

Four of hearts   jack of clubs

Scourge   Cross

Home   Strength

We read the four corners from the entrance card in a clockwise circle or Scourge, Cross, Strength and Home. Returning troubles, heavy repeated burdens make Frank stronger and family and friends. Home knighting to High Tower indicates that this Home card is largely about being isolated from family and friends in his location and being forced to find new friends and supporters. These four corners tell us this will be a hard uphill slog for Frank for quite some time should he choose to accept this challenge and relocate.

Now we mirror Home and Cross indicating that Frank will repeatedly feel home sick and miss his family and friends for some time. We can also mirror Scourge and Strength which indicates Frank manifesting strength in the midst of constant, relentless trials.

We can also mirror across the three of spades or Scourge and seven of clubs or Cross. If Frank has previously had a drinking or drug problem, then this could possibly indicate the return of this problem due to the stresses of his new environment. If Frank had no addiction problems previously, then this new job and environment will prove to be a constant trial to Frank.

Finally, we mirror four of hearts or Home and jack of clubs and Strength which indicates that moving away from home makes Frank a stronger person because he now has to stand on his own, and his friends and family are far away, so he has to make all these decisions on his own. This combination can also indicate that Frank is very attached to his family and friends and home and has very strong feeling about leaving them. It's much harder for him to spend hours discussing all these things with his family due to schedules and distance. He's on his own in a new world.

In conclusion, I think this work relocation move for Frank although difficult both personally and professionally will not turn out to be a disaster. This relocation will also not result in an improved work environment, more money or opportunities for Frank as he hopes. Perhaps he might consider some other alternatives to accepting this transfer and he could cast the cards on each alternative until he can come up with some better options.

Chapter 11

THE 4 ACES SPREAD

THE 15 CARD 4 ACES SPREAD

The four aces spread is a fifteen card reading and each of the four aces represents a different area of the seekers life. Even though this is a large reading with many cards and multiple areas of the seekers life represented, a clear question written down before casting the cards will provide the best advice. The energy of each ace contains the potential energy of all of the cards in its suit.

STEP 1 – Remove the four aces with your meanings written upon them from your practice deck.

STEP 2 – Place these four aces in a square pattern.

STEP 3 – Write down your question and shuffle your seekers deck while focusing on this question.

STEP 4 – Cast your cards in groups of three beneath each ace from your practice deck.

Ace of hearts	Ace of clubs
CARD 1/ 2/ 3	CARD 4/ 5/ 6

Outcome
CARD 7/ 8/ 9

Ace of diamonds	Ace of spades
CARD 10/ 11/ 12	CARD 13/ 14/ 15

MEANING OF EACH GROUP

Ace of hearts – cards 1, 2 and 3 in this group represent matters of the heart including love relationships, family, God and spiritual life.

Ace of diamonds – cards 10, 11 and 12 in this group represent finances, communication, business and the physical world.

Ace of clubs – cards 4, 5 and 6 in this group represent the seekers foundation, connections and rooted-ness.

Ace of spades – cards 13, 14 and 15 in this group represent conflict, challenges, decisions, endings and obstacles.

The three cards in the center – represent the destiny line or the outcome of the current situation unless the seeker takes action to change it.

EXAMPLE – FOUR ACES SPREAD

Tina is 39 years young and divorced for a year after fifteen years of marriage. She has two children from her ex husband and maintains primary custody. Tina asks, "Will I marry again?"

Ace of hearts
Six of diamonds/ five of spades/ six of hearts
Hand in Hand/ Road Block/ Karmic Relationship

Ace of clubs
Nine of clubs/ four of clubs/ six of spades
High Tower/ Four Leaf Clover/ Incubus-Succubus

Ace of diamonds
Eight of hearts/ jack of clubs/ eight of spades
Water into Wine/ Strength/ Scapegoat

Ace of spades
Ten of spades/ nine of diamonds/ two of spades
Earthquake/ Mercury/ Broken Chalice

Outcome
Three of clubs/ nine of hearts/ two of hearts
Three Black Birds/ Yes/ Lovers

The **Ace of Hearts** section represents matters of the heart including love relationships, family, God and spiritual life. This is a love question, so I will expect to find some very important cards in this section. Tina cast the six of diamonds, five of spades and six of hearts or Hand in Hand, Road Block and Karmic Relationship. This reads that new relationships (Hand in Hand) are blocked (Road Block) by her previous long term relationship (Karmic Relationship). So even though Tina wants to begin dating again and move forward with her life, she is feeling emotionally blocked (ace of hearts) by her recent divorce. It's common to have unhealed wounds and emotional hurts from a divorce.

The **Ace of Clubs** section represents the seekers foundation, connections and rooted-ness. Tina cast the nine of clubs, four of clubs and six of spades or High Tower, Four Leaf Clover and Incubus-Succubus. Since the divorce, Tina has isolated herself from relationships due to her marriage going toxic as indicated by High Tower and Incubus-Succubus. However four of clubs or Four Leaf Clover says she is beginning to feel alive again and is beginning to rebuild her foundation. The four of clubs or Four Leaf Clover is also a card of activity and action, so we see that new activity is beginning to sprout in this area. We can also sum these three cards in this section to arrive at 19. Nine of clubs, four of clubs and six of spades = 9+4+6= 19. 19 = five of clubs or Crossroads. This advises that it is time for Tina to get back out onto the Crossroads into the world and leave her High Tower where she has been healing.

The **Ace of diamonds** section represents the physical world and the abundance of life. Tina cast the eight of hearts, jack of clubs and eight of spades or Water into Wine, Strength and Scapegoat. Interestingly, no diamonds suited cards appeared in this section for her question. The eight of hearts and the eight of spades are opposite energies and the jack of clubs is Strength. Tina has a very strong desire to re-enter the world and make a fresh start at life (Water into Wine and Strength) but her world has been shattered by her divorce (Scapegoat) and she feels hurt and damaged in every possible area of her existence. We can also sum these three cards to arrive at 27. Eight of hearts, jack of club and eight of spades = 8+11+8= 27 or the seven of clubs or Cross. The Cross here indicates that Tina feels burdened by this long trial of divorce. Cross pairs here with Strength and indicates that this has made Tina a much stronger person.

The **Ace of spades** section represents conflict, challenges, decisions, endings and obstacles. Tina cast the ten of spades, nine of diamonds and two of spades or Earthquake, Mercury and Broken Chalice. Here we get more insight into Tina's divorce in this section. Earthquake and Broken Chalice indicate that Tina's divorce completely devastated her life. Mercury moves very fast indicating that these events occurred with great speed. In an instant, Tina's entire life changed dramatically. Adding these three cards we arrive at 21. 10+9+2 = 21 or the six of hearts meaning Karmic Relationship. The Karmic Relationship represented here is her marriage. The sudden ending of her marriage by divorce (Karmic Relationship and Broken Chalice) completely changed her life in an instant (Earthquake and Mercury).

The **Outcome** section represents the outcome of the current situation unless the seeker takes action to change it. Tina cast the three of clubs, nine of hearts and two of hearts or Three Black Birds, Yes and Lovers. Three Black Birds is a very social card and indicates interacting with groups of people in social situations. Great news, despite all the issues and recent divorce, the answer is yes, Tina will get her wish to remarry if she chooses and all that is required is for her to get back out there on the dating scene until she finds the right man.

Summary- The four aces spread gives a very detailed view of the situation and the factors affecting the question and the seeker providing the seeker an abundance of information and advice with regard to choosing the best way forward.

Chapter 12

THE 54 CARD GRAND TABLET OF THE MAGUS

THE GRAND TABLET OF THE MAGUS

The grand tablet of the magus is the grand daddy of all playing card spreads and employs the use of all fifty four cards. The grand tablet of the magus provides the "big picture" of everything going on in the seekers life or a snapshot of all inputs and outputs occurring related to any question asked by the seeker.

The grand tablet of the magus is a very advanced spreading technique and uses all of the previous techniques we have learned up until this point and some very new and powerful ones including reading the houses.

The grand tablet of the magus employs both the practice deck and seeker's deck. We will cast the first the practice deck in order of appearance in this book and next we will shuffle the seeker's deck while centering ourselves and thinking about our question. We will then cast our seeker's deck cards one by one on top of the practice deck already laid out.

STEP 1: Cast the practice deck in six rows of nine according to "Exhibit A."

Exhibit A

CARDS 1/ 2/ 3/ 4/ 5/ 6/ 7/ 8/ 9
10/ 11/ 12/ 13/ 14/ 15/ 16/ 17/ 18
19/ 20/ 21/ 22/ 23/ 24/ 25/ 26/ 27
28/ 29/ 30/ 31/ 32/ 33/ 34/ 35/ 36
37/ 38/ 39/ 40/ 41/ 42/ 43/ 44/ 45
46/ 47/ 48/ 49/ 50/ 51/ 52/ 53/ 54

Lay the practice deck cards down according to the order in Exhibit A. Each card in your practice deck now represents a "house" or the energy of the seekers card after landing there. (ABBR = "abbreviation" of playing card)

Exhibit B
CARD/ ABBR./ HOUSE
1. Ace of hearts/ Ah/ Heart
2. Ace of diamonds/ Ad/ Sun
3. Ace of clubs/ Ac/ Mustard Seed
4. Ace of spades/ As/ Straight Razor
5. Two of hearts/ 2h/ Lovers
6. Two of diamonds/ 2d/ Diamond Ring
7. Two of clubs/ 2c/ Handcuffs
8. Two of spades/ 2s/ Broken Chalice
9. Three of hearts/ 3h/ Roses
10. Three of diamonds/ 3d/Trinity
11. Three of clubs/ 3c/ 3 Black Birds
12. Three of spades/ 3s/ Scourge
13. Four of hearts/ 4h/ Home
14. Four of diamonds/ 4d/ Cornerstone
15. Four of clubs/ 4c/ Four Leaf Clover
16. Four of spades/ 4s/ Coffin
17. Five of hearts/ 5h/ Fence Sitter
18. Five of diamonds/ 5d/ Jacob's Ladder
19. Five of clubs/ 5c/ Crossroads
20. Five of spades/ 5s/ Road Block
21. Six of hearts/ 6h/ Karmic Relationship
22. Six of diamonds/ 6d/ Hand in Hand
23. Six of clubs/ 6c/ Olive Tree
24. Six of spades/ 6s/ Incubus-Succubus
25. Seven of hearts/ 7h/ Stars
26. Seven of diamonds/ 7d/ Finger of God
27. Seven of clubs/ 7c/ Cross
28. Seven of spades/ 7s/ Veil
29. Eight of hearts/ 8h/ Water into Wine
30. Eight of diamonds/ 8d/ Cornucopia
31. Eight of clubs/8c/ City
32. Eight of spades/ 8s/ Scapegoat
33. Nine of hearts/ 9h/ Yes
34. Nine of diamonds/ 9d/ Mercury
35. Nine of clubs/ 9c/ High Tower
36. Nine of spades/ 9s/ No
37. Ten of hearts/ 10h/ Cup Overflowing
38. Ten of diamonds/ 10d/ Inheritance
39. Ten of clubs/ 10c/ Hamster Wheel

40. Ten of spades/ 10s/ Earthquake
41. Jack of hearts/ Jh/ Angel
42. Jack of diamonds/ Jd/ Player
43. Jack of clubs/ Jc/ Strength
44. Jack of spades/ Js/ Devil
45. Queen of hearts/ Qh/ Woman
46. Queen of diamonds/ Qd/ Fox
47. Queen of clubs/ Qc/ Mother Earth
48. Queen of spades/ Qs/ Snake
49. King of hearts/ Kh/ Man
50. King of diamonds/ Kd/ Magi
51. King of clubs/ Kc/ Ruler
52. King of spades/ Ks/ Judge
53. Red joker/ Rj/ Butterfly
54. Black joker/ Bj/ Karmic Shift

David's mother is 86 years old and his two siblings recently moved her into a nursing home. David's father passed away fifteen years earlier. She suffers from a recurrence of breast cancer thirty years after the first occurrence which resulted in a double mastectomy. She has become unable to care for herself and is in need of around the clock care. Both of David's older siblings still live within close driving distance of the family home and his mother. David is the black sheep who couldn't wait to get away and has lived everywhere around the country except his home state since he was age seventeen. David is now forty nine years old. He has not maintained a close relationship with his family.

David is wondering about his mother's health and if his mother's death is near. He gets regular updates on the health of his mother but those are laced with copious amounts of guilt and recrimination and he doesn't know how much is true and how much is melodramatic guilt mongering. There is also some property that will pass through her will. It has been stated frankly to him that he will receive none of it due to his absence from the family. He is financially very sound but he also questions the truth of those statements.

David shuffles and casts the following grand tablet of the magus using all 54 cards on this situation with his mother and family. The tableau is cast in 7 rows of 9 cards each until all 54 cards are cast. I have abbreviated the card names and listed their positions 1-54 in order that the relationships between the cards can be visually examined. I encourage you, the reader, to lay out your practice deck in order of the houses and seekers deck in the random casting order so that it will be easier to follow along. Random Seekers order cast on top of the practice deck below.

Exhibit C
1- Js/ 2-10c/ 3-Qh/ 4-Kc/ 5-9c/ 6-3s/ 7-8c/ 8-8s/ 9-7c
10-Kd/11-5c/12-4s/13-6d/14-Ks/15-Ad/16-Bj/17-Ac/18-9h
19-8h/ 20-4c/21-2c/22-Qs/23-Jc/24-5s/25-6c/26-8d/27-Jd
28-As/29-Jh/30-3d/31-6h/32-6s/33-4d/34-7s/35-2h/36-3h
37-4h/38-9d/39-3c/40-Ah/41-2s/42-9s/43-10s/44-5d/45-Rj
46-10h/47-5h/48-10d/49-7d/50-Qc/51-Kh/52-7h/53-2d/54-Qd

The best way to learn a new spreading technique is by real life example. We will read the grand tablet of the magus in the following order using these steps:

STEP 1: Read the houses. The subject of David's tableau is his mother. His mother will most naturally be the queen of hearts or the Woman card since she is the subject of the spread. David will naturally be the king of hearts or the Man card since it is his tableau. Additionally, before casting this tableau, David charged the queen of hearts to represent his mother by simply telling (or commanding) the deck that the queen of hearts would represent his mother. The queen of hearts falls in house #3 or under the energy of the ace of clubs meaning Mustard Seed. The Woman card landing in the house of Mustard Seed indicates that a new phase of life is beginning for her and her situation is about to change dramatically.

The king of hearts or Man representing David is in house #51, the house of king of clubs or Ruler. The Ruler is the boss man. He is in charge. The fact that David falls in this house means that he is in the driver's seat in this relationship with his mother and his family. The other thing that I notice is that Man and Woman or David and his mother are very far apart in the spread and are not connecting directly. Also, I see that the king of clubs is right next to the queen of hearts. The king of clubs or Ruler is in house #4 ace of spades or Straight Razor indicating that David and his mother essentially don't communicate and have a severed relationship. They are not emotionally close and this likely also indicates serious conflict between them. The king of hearts or Man is at the bottom of the spread. This positioning of the card representing David indicates that the circumstances described by this GT are happening to him and weighing down on him more so than initiated by him. The Man card landing at the bottom also indicates that the cycle of events described here are ending for David and he is about to enter into a new cycle beyond the scope of this current GT casting. David's mother contrarily sits at the top of this GT casting as the queen of hearts or Woman card which indicates that she is at the beginning of a new cycle. The Woman card falling in position #3 ace of clubs or Mustard Seed emphasizes this fact.

Another card we want to look at is the eight of spades or the Scapegoat. Scapegoat represents any serious physical illness, especially any illness like cancer that has spread throughout the body through metastasis. We find the Scapegoat in house #8 two of spades or the Broken Chalice. Both Scapegoat and Broken Chalice are separation and alienation cards which likely emphasize the fact that David's mother is very ill at this point and may even indicate that her spirit is literally beginning the process of separating from her physical body.

Another card we want to look at is the four of spades or Coffin. We find Coffin in house #12 the three of spades or Scourge indicating recurring pain as well as that this illness will ultimately result in death.

Another card to look at is the four of hearts or Family. We find this card in house #37 the ten of hearts or Cup Overflowing. Cup Overflowing is about satisfaction and happiness. This indicates that the close family is very supportive in her illness. Ten of hearts indicates that they are being as supportive and helpful as they possibly can. Let's look for David's sister who will be represented here as the queen of diamonds or Fox. We find Fox in house #54 Karmic Shift. This indicates that David's sister's previous unconcerned attitude has dramatically shifted since her mother has entered the nursing home and she has really stepped up to the plate to care for the details of her mother's circumstances as she makes sure to tell David every time she calls.

There are so many cards we can look at in their houses and as a rule, I choose the topics of greatest interest before casting the tableau and designate the representative cards by command. One last card that strikes me here is that the jack of spades or Devil appears in house #1 the ace of hearts or Heart. Since this is a health reading, this very likely indicates a serious problem with her heart which had not come up in previous discussions with David's family.

STEP 2: Read Past, present and future. Since this is a reading on David's mother's health and Woman is in house #3, the past is represented by the cards to the left of the Woman card or ten of clubs and jack of spades or Hamster Wheel and Devil. Her past may be read as a very difficult journey for the mother. She's feeling trapped. She's getting sicker and sicker. Her future is represented by the cards to her right or king of clubs, nine of clubs, three of spades, eight of clubs, eight of spades and seven of clubs or Ruler, High Tower, Scourge, City, Scapegoat and Cross. The High Tower here is nursing home or formal medical establishment. This may read Kc, 9c, she's under the care of doctors and living in the nursing home 3s, 8c, 8s, 7c- experiencing a lot of pain and with two eights present on the line (eights are very global cards affecting everything represented by that energy) this is her world now. City, Scapegoat and Cross indicate everything all at once going wrong with her health. There are no sunny, getting better cards in her future. It's worth noting the end of her future line is the Cross representing the cross of Jesus Christ and therefore the afterlife, the spiritual world and death. It's also worth noting that Cross falls in house #9 the three of hearts or Roses. When God, Angels, the Holy Spirit and mother Mary visit on the earth from the spirit realm they come with the fragrance of Roses. Contrarily, when fallen angels, demons or unclean spirits manifest they often come with the smell of rotting flesh, sulfur and human excrement.

We can also read from the Woman position down and up. There is no up here since Woman sits in house #3 at the top of the tableau indicating that she is beginning a new cycle as previously mentioned. Down reads four of spades, two of clubs, three of diamonds, three of clubs and ten of diamonds or Coffin, Handcuffs, Trinity, 3 Black Birds and Inheritance. Again, the line ends with Inheritance, a card of completion and reward. The Bible describes death as the receiving of the inheritance. The Woman sits right atop the Coffin card indicating that death is knocking on her door. This line can be read as the Woman is connected 2c to 4s death 3d, 3c, 10d and everything is working toward completion and a final summing up of her life.

We should also read the diagonals radiating from the Woman card. The diagonal to the left reads queen of hearts, five of clubs and eight of hearts or Woman, Crossroads and Water into Wine. Again, the last card in this line is Water into Wine; a card indicating transformation. Water into Wine is an eight indicating that this transformation will affect everything. Water into Wine sits in house #19 the five of clubs or Crossroads indicating a journey of transformation. This line may be read as the Woman will move out onto the Crossroads to begin a journey of transformation or literally transitioning from the physical world into the after life.

The diagonal radiating down and to the right of the Woman card reads queen of hearts, six of diamonds, jack of clubs, four of diamonds, ten of spades and two of diamonds or Woman, Hand in Hand, Strength, Cornerstone, Earthquake and Diamond Ring. This line ends with Diamond Ring a union card. Diamond Ring sits in house #53 or Butterfly. Again, what says transformation more clearly than the ugly caterpillar in human form transforming into the beautiful Butterfly? Ten of spades or Earthquake indicates that the old order of existence will be completely destroyed to reveal this new situation and union with transformation. The line additionally reads

Hand in Hand, Strength and Cornerstone. Hand in Hand sits in House #13 the four of hearts or Home which indicates many helpers. These helpers are karmic relationships or angels, but they are family in the truest sense of the word whether they were represented here on earth in physical form in this incarnation or not. Strength sits in house #23 the six of clubs or Olive Tree indicating to me that she is part of something much bigger than herself which is enduring and has very deep roots. Finally, Cornerstone sits in house #33 the nine of hearts or Yes. Nine of hearts or Yes is again a very transformational card, also known as the open door or the key. This new reality exists beyond the gate, reminding me of the gates of heaven or through the open door. There exists here a lot of information in this reading about the afterlife indicating that these are the next steps for David's mother and that time is short if David wishes to reconcile his relationship.

Reading David's past events lines from the king of hearts or Man card we find the king of hearts, queen of clubs, seven of diamonds, ten of diamonds, five of hearts and ten of hearts in his past or Man, Mother Earth, Finger of God, Inheritance, Fence Sitter and Cup Overflowing. Remember David, age forty nine, left home at age seventeen and has only been back very briefly since and has not visited at all for more than ten years. This line indicates that David has established himself, has had success materially and financially, and the ten of hearts or Cup Overflowing indicates that he couldn't be happier with where his life stands now. Cup Overflowing sits in house #46 the queen of hearts or Fox. In this case, Fox would be a card of business and making shrewd decisions.

David's future line reads king of hearts, seven of hearts, two of diamonds and queen of diamonds or Man,

Stars, Diamond Ring and Fox. This line indicates healing of his relationship 7h with his mother. Seven of hearts is also the return of love card and this card is followed by Diamond Ring indicating reconnection with his family and his mother.

Let's read David's diagonals proceeding up since the king of heart or Man card sits at the bottom of the tableau indicating that David is at the end of a cycle as read in his past line. Reading diagonally up to the left we have king of hearts, two of spades, six of hearts, two of clubs, five of clubs and jack of spades or Man, Broken Chalice, Karmic Relationship, Handcuffs, Crossroads and Devil. The line ends with Devil in House #1 the ace of hearts or Heart house. There are some bitter feelings and circumstances surrounding David's departure from family life. Reading the rest of the line from Man we have the two of spades and the six of hearts (Broken Chalice and Karmic Relationship) indicating a broken Karmic Relationship or family relationship. The two of clubs or Handcuffs card is a relationship with no feelings. David feels obligated to his family and bound to them with Handcuffs. Crossroads and Devil indicate that he is feeling trapped and obligated to go out to see them. David seems not terribly excited to see his family and the only reason he is willing to go there at this point looks like guilt.

Reading David's diagonal up to the right we find the king of hearts, ten of spades, two of hearts and jack of diamonds or Man, Earthquake, Lovers and Player. This line ends with Player. Player sits in house #27 the seven of clubs or Cross. The Player is literally a new man or situation and Cross can be a burden, extended period of tribulation or religious faith. Player in house of Cross reads either David is a new man due to renewed faith in God which will directly affect his decisions regarding his family or a new and greater burden will soon reveal itself directly affecting David's life. The rest of the line from Man reads ten of spades and two of hearts (Earthquake and Lovers) that the love relationship was devastated and destroyed (Player) leading to a very independent way of life for David. The Earthquake card sits in house #43 the jack of clubs or Strength meaning this ending had a powerful effect in David's life and on the relationship. The Lovers sits in house #35 the nine of clubs or High Tower meaning that the effect of these events resulted in David separating and moving far away from his family. David confirms that he has recently had a renewal of faith and is praying regularly and begun attending church after an extended absence. This line also indicates that the situation with his mother's health may change very soon.

STEP 3: Distance. How far are the Man and Woman cards from each other in the spread? If they are close to each other or on the same line with each other or connect through knighting, then this would indicate a closer connection. In this tableau we see that Man and Woman do not connect directly in a line, by knighting and they sit on opposite ends of a very large card spread. The Man and Woman here are both physically and emotionally very far apart.

STEP 4: Meeting points of major cards – in this case Man and Woman. Follow the line from the king of hearts straight up to the three of spades or Scourge. Now follow the line from the queen of hearts straight down to the ten of diamonds or Inheritance. So, although the Man and Woman do not directly connect in this spread, their meeting points are Scourge and Inheritance indicating ongoing conflict and either a literal inheritance to be passed at death or simply that they are from the same family line. Summing up to this point we find that David and his mother are very far apart physically and emotionally, there is an abundance of ongoing conflict in their relationship and the main connection really comes down to a blood relationship at this point.

STEP 5: Read the first five cards (houses one through four) which provide the "main issue" or "theme" of the tableau. We have already read the first five cards since the Woman card sits in position #3 on the first line. The first five cards read the jack of spades, ten of clubs, queen of hearts, king of clubs and nine of clubs or Devil, Hamster Wheel, Woman, Ruler and High Tower. We read five cards because we can mirror and pair the cards as we learned previously with the five card position-less spread. These lines may be read as a very difficult and long journey for the Woman puts her into Kc, 9c a nursing home. That's definitely accurate. Nine of clubs is often a hospital or official building and the Ruler or king of clubs is in control there. Ten of clubs of Hamster Wheel mirrors king of clubs or Ruler indicating the entire journey is under the control of this powerful person. Devil mirrors High Tower indicating that this is a very serious, very pernicious illness requiring hospitalization and extended rest.

STEP 6: Read the last five cards (houses fifty through fifty four) which provide the "fate line" or "outcome" of this current picture unless free will actions are taken to intentionally change this outcome. Unusually, we have also previously read these cards in this tableau for the Man's future line. Nevertheless, they read queen of clubs, king of hearts, seven of hearts, two of diamonds and queen of diamonds or Earth Mother, Man, Star, Diamond

Ring and Fox. This line can be read healing for the man through union with a woman. The Star card also indicates the return of a love relationship and suggests David reuniting with his family. The two queens mirror each other here emphasizing the strong female influence and the king of hearts mirrors the two of hearts indicating the Man reconnecting with loved ones or family.

STEP 7: Draw boxes of nine cards around major cards. Here, the two cards around which we will make a square of nine are the king of hearts or Man and queen of hearts or Woman, however, you may do a nine square around any major topic card. Choose the representative card(s) before casting the spread and command the deck accordingly. Always place the subject card as close to the center of the other eight cards chosen as possible. Here, the king of hearts sits on the last row, so he will be on the bottom, center of this square of nine cards.

6s Incubus-Succubus/ 4d Cornerstone/ 7s Veil
2s Broken Chalice/ 9s No/ 10s Earthquake
Qc Earth Mother/ Kh Man/ 7h Star

See how I formed the square of nine around the Man card? Normally, I would place him in the space occupied by the nine of spades, but Man sits on the bottom line of the tableau, so instead he is placed at the bottom, center of the square of nine. Always place the significant card as close to the center of the square of nine as possible depending on it's natural place in the GT.

We can use all of the previously learned techniques on this nine square including entrance and exit, center theme, knighting, mirroring and past, present, future.

Past line down reads six of spades, two of spades and queen of clubs or Incubus-Succubus, Broken Chalice and Earth Mother. We may read this as toxic relationships resulted in David divorcing him self from the situation. The past line across reads the six of spades, four of diamonds and seven of spades or Incubus-Succubus, Cornerstone and Veil and we may read this as a long history of toxic relationships and buried and hidden pain in the foundation of the family.

Present line down reads four of diamonds, nine of spades and king of hearts or Cornerstone, No and Man. We may interpret this as David remains completely separated from this foundation or his family and home. The No or nine of spades in the center represents a full stop of the relationship and very accurately portrays the current situation between David and his family. Present line across reads two of spades, nine of spades and ten of spades or Broken Chalice, No and Earthquake. We may read this as major events and broken relationships completely severed David's connection with his family. This is a very dark line and we can see how serious is the rift between David and his family.

Future line down reads seven of spades, ten of spades and seven of hearts or Veil, Earthquake and Star. We may read this as the mothers illness results in Earthquake - a world changing event and healing within the family. I would interpret combination of Veil and Earthquake here as the likely death of David's mother and her passing into the next world. Her death will be very traumatic for all concerned and perhaps most of all for David himself as well as really shake up the family structure since David's father has already passed several years prior. Star is also the exit card, so this box of nine ends on a message of hope while the entrance card is Incubus-Succubus indicating how toxic these relationships have become in the intervening years. Future line across gives a little more hope and reads queen of clubs, king of hearts and seven of hearts or Earth Mother, Man and Star. We may read this as David will find healing in the entire situation with his family.

The Man card knights six of spades or Incubus-Succubus and seven of spades or Veil. This knighting emphasizes the very long history of conflict toxicity and buried pain present in his family relationships which caused him to simply give up and cut them off completely.

There's much more we can read from just this square of nine, but this is mostly a repetition of information we have already gleaned from other areas of the tableau.

A nine square for the mother will read:

10c Hamster Wheel/ Qh Woman/   Kc Ruler
5c Crossroads/   4s Coffin/   6d Hand in Hand
4c 4 Leaf Clover/ 2c Handcuffs/ Qs Snake

As before, I prefer that the Woman card land in the space occupied by the Coffin card, however, the Woman sits on the first line of the tableau, so she lands in the center, top row of the square rather than the middle.

Past line down reads the ten of clubs, five of clubs and four of clubs or Hamster Wheel, Crossroads and 4 Leaf Clover. Look at all those foundational club cards! We may interpret this to read mom traveled a very long road in life and had good luck with her health until finally at a very advanced age, her luck ran out and she has come to a Crossroads. She is 86 years old. Past line across reads ten of clubs, queen of hearts and king of clubs or Hamster

Wheel, Woman and Ruler. We may interpret this as the Woman was in complete control of her faculties and life journey in the past. Hamster Wheel often represents a long journey and also represents the long journey of life itself. So many clubs in these lines also indicates that the Woman enjoyed a solid foundation of good health for most of her life until very recently.

Present line down reads queen of hearts, four of spades and two of clubs or Woman, Coffin and Handcuffs. The Woman here literally sits on top of the Coffin and the Handcuffs indicate a picture of binding her inevitably to this result. The Coffin card also sits right in the center of this nine square and represents the theme of this reading. This indicates to me that she is very close to death as previously stated. Present line across reads five of clubs, four of spades and six of diamonds or Crossroads, Coffin and Hand in Hand. We may interpret this as those on the other side of the veil are standing at the Crossroads ready to lead her across to the other side. This can also be interpreted that there are many on this side helping to bring her to this final result including health care workers and David's siblings.

Future line down reads king of clubs, six of diamonds and queen of spades or Ruler, Hand in Hand and Snake. The Snake here represents a serious illness like cancer that wraps itself around all the organs of the body, especially in a health reading. So I read this line as this illness will finally take control of everything in her body and declare itself king of the realm, ultimately killing the host.

The queen of spades or Snake knights to the queen of hearts or Woman and five of clubs or Crossroads also indicating that this Snake sends the Woman out to the Crossroads and onto a new path. The center card and theme is four of spades meaning Coffin or death. Queen of spades is also the exit card and holds a particularly powerful position in this square of nine.

That essentially covers the major points to reading a grand tablet of the magus. There is more we can do with this magnificent spread. Furthermore, a tableau on a subject should not be cast more than once a month because the situation will simply not change enough to warrant another complete examination. Also, a good tableau should be pondered for about a month to really see all the relationships and messages present for the seeker.

Chapter 13

THE 10 CARD CELTIC CROSS POSITIONAL SPREAD

The Celtic cross ten cards lay out is enduringly one of the most popular spreads to use for card divination. The Celtic cross spread provides a lot of background information about a situation as well as several possible outcome cards making it a must have in the card diviners arsenal. The Celtic cross layout is most popular amongst tarot readers; however any card spread utilized by tarot readers may be adopted and used with playing cards and vice versa.

Rachel's high school sweetheart, who she hasn't spoken to in fifteen years, has recently divorced and has befriended her on Facebook. He has been personal messaging her and trying to reconnect. She hasn't responded yet and is wondering, "What are his intentions? Is he looking for a relationship or just comfort in his divorce?"

Lay the cards out in this order and pattern:

```
                10
         5       9
   4    1,2  6   8
         3       7
```

THE CELTIC CROSS POSITION MEANINGS

The Celtic cross may be read with various position meanings, but ultimately they are fairly consistent among most readers. These are the positions I find to be simplest, most useful and common.

CARD 1 - HEART OF THE MATTER. The central issue; the theme or primary issue.

CARD 2 – WHAT IS CROSSING. This card is literally laid across the first card. Card 2 indicates the opposing element; what lies in opposition to the main theme; important relevant information.

CARD 3 – BASIS. Foundation upon which these events are built; the root cause; the source.

CARD 4 – PAST. Recent events affecting this situation.

CARD 5 – PRESSING ISSUE. On the mind; needing immediate attention; possibilities.

CARD 6 – NEAR FUTURE. Next logical results of current actions; coming attractions dictated by this branch of actions; arriving immediately upon the scene and this new information and change of situation may or may not be already revealed to seeker.

CARD 7 – SELF. The true self revealed in this situation; what's really going on in the head and life of the person under examination.

CARD 8 – PEOPLE AND EVENTS. Actions and events occurring in the environment affecting this situation whether known or unknown to the seeker or participants.

CARD 9 – HOPES & FEARS. That which the seeker hopes or fears will occur.

CARD 10 – OUTCOME. The place where all of this is leading; the resolution to the current events as they stand without free will action to change the results.

Rachel's high school sweetheart Tom, who she hasn't spoken to in fifteen years, has recently divorced and has befriended her on Facebook. He has been personal messaging her and trying to reconnect. She hasn't responded yet and is wondering, "What are his intentions? Is he looking for a relationship or just comfort in his divorce?"

Rachael shuffles and casts:

CARD 1 - Three of diamonds; Trinity
CARD 2 - Nine of clubs; High Tower
CARD 3 – Eight of spades; Scapegoat
CARD 4 - Five of spades; Roadblock
CARD 5 - Seven of spades; Veil
CARD 6 – Three of hearts; Roses
CARD 7 – King of spades; Executioner
CARD 8 – Five of diamonds; Jacob's Ladder
CARD 9 – Ace of diamonds; Sun
CARD 10 – Nine of diamonds; Mercury

CARD 1 – HEART OF THE MATTER. The three of diamonds or Trinity. Threes are an indication of increase and improvement. The three of diamonds or Trinity indicates that Tom is trying to improve his situation or start building on the new foundation. Tom's intentions therefore are not casual sex, but he is thinking of Rachel as part of his new foundation. So far, this is a good sign and showing potential.

CARD 2 – WHAT IS CROSSING. The nine of clubs or High Tower indicating that Tom is now single as he says. His divorce is complete or he is at least emotionally separate from his ex wife and he's again a free man. Reading High Tower paired with Trinity indicates that he is now trying to rebuild as a newly single man.

CARD 3 – BASIS. The eight of spades or Scapegoat is often a card of major illness and could indicate that Tom feels like he's the big loser in the divorce; that he was painted as the villain, used and discarded as the scapegoat by his ex wife in the process of freeing herself from the bonds of marriage. Scapegoat in the basis position indicates that Tom is feeling pretty low after his divorce. He feels like he barely survived a disaster.

CARD 4 – PAST. The five of spades or Road Block appears in the past position indicating that Tom is still feeling blocked and having trouble getting around recent events in his life. This divorce was a big deal and quite traumatic for him.

CARD 5 – PRESSING ISSUE. The seven of spades or Veil appears in this position. Sevens are cards of return and the seven of spades is something unconscious or hidden; history, unprocessed karma and emotions that return again and again until the recipient has finally processed it. In this case, the Veil indicates that Tom is either psychologically obsessing over all the regrets of his recent divorce, there are a million unpleasant details yet to be worked out or a little of both. Either way, Tom's mind is constantly returning to the dark well of his recent divorce, regret and all the many losses and problems associated with it.

So far, this is a fairly dark spread. Tom is at a low point in his life and trying to begin to rebuild with the three of diamonds or Trinity in the heart of the matter position. Aces stand alone, twos are a couple and the number three of any suit is the first attempts at building something from scratch. The three of diamonds or Trinity is about trying to cobble together a new material foundation (diamonds suit). Tom is newly single and feeling maybe a little lonely as represented by the nine of clubs or High Tower. Next come the eight of spades, five of spades and seven of spades or Scapegoat, Road Block and Veil indicating a triple play of pain, frustration and obsessive negative regretful thinking and circumstances.

CARD 6 – NEAR FUTURE. The three of hearts or Roses appears in this position. Tom is going to make future romantic overtures to Rachel. Another three in this position is a good sign as three indicates building something. Tom is climbing out of the emotional ditch he's fallen into.

CARD 7 – SELF. The king of spades or Executioner appears in the self position. This indicates that Tom is currently having a very dark view of himself. He's the scapegoat (eight of spades) and made out to be the "bad guy" in the divorce and he's internalized this and is feeling really hurt by the judgments made against him. Alternatively, the Executioner in this position could mean that Tom feels that he took decisive action to do what needed to be done to end the pain and frustration of his marriage. My read here is that so many spades in previous positions indicates the former and that he is very literally in a dark mood or currently in a dark place.

CARD 8 – PEOPLE AND EVENTS. The five of diamonds or Jacob's Ladder appears in the people and events position. Jacob's Ladder often appears when someone has reached rock bottom and there is nowhere to go but up. Tom is rebuilding his life and actively taking steps to improve his lot.

It's worth noting that there are four diamonds and four spades in this spread of ten cards. There is only one heart card and one club suited card. For a love spread, there are precious few hearts represented. Spades are conflict and negative emotion cards and diamonds are very solid material situation and communication cards. From this distribution of suits, we may conclude that actions are stalled between Rachel and Tom and there's been no opportunity yet for emotions to develop between them. This is accurate, since Rachel has not responded to any of Tom's personal messages.

CARD 9 – HOPES & FEARS. The ace of diamonds or Sun appears in the Hopes & Fears position indicating that Rachael hopes for a long term successful relationship with Tom. That Tom will just "get over it" and move on. Tom is going to continue going through the agony of divorce both in his mind and with the endless details of working out interactions with his children and handling his currently toxic relationship with his ex wife. The Sun card in this position advises Rachel to give Tom room to talk about this situation as needed and air it out so that he doesn't feel stuck dealing with it on his own, on his own time.

CARD 10 – OUTCOME. The nine of diamonds or Mercury appears in the outcome position. Mercury was the lightening fast winged messenger of the gods and therefore this is primarily a card of communication. Tom will contact Rachel again very soon. Based on all this new information, Rachel needs to decide if she wants to respond and see where this goes. Tom is not looking for a quick hook up with Rachel but a real connection. However, he is suffering from a little bit of drowning man syndrome at this point in his journey through life. The distribution of spades verses diamonds indicates that Tom will likely pull through this dark period fairly quickly and get back on track. There is a lot of pain and trouble in Tom's life currently which can't be ignored and is part of the package.

Chapter 14

JOURNALING

As a rule, I don't like to use the words "never" or "always" however, always write down the questions, the cards cast in your spreads with the positions and, of course, the answers given. This will help you learn faster and you will have a physical record of the progression of advice given as you travel through these seasons of life.

It is also possible to keep electronic records of spreads with photos and email and other electronic documents. I also use these methods as a supplement to a hand written journal and know many others who solely use electronic records. I recommend electronic records be employed only as a supplement to a physical, hand written journal. This journal is by far the most useful tool in my arsenal aside from the cards themselves.

Made in the USA
Columbia, SC
17 May 2021

38060950R00107